THE
GLAM SCAM

To those who didn't deserve to be victims—E.J.

THE
GLAM SCAM

Successfully avoiding

the casting couch

and other talent and

modeling scams.

ERIK JOSEPH

Lone Eagle Publishing Company
Los Angeles, California

THE GLAM SCAM: Successfully Avoiding the Casting Couch and Other Talent and Modeling Scams

Copyright © 1994 by Erik Joseph

LONE EAGLE PUBLISHING COMPANY
2337 Roscomare Road, Suite Nine
Los Angeles, CA 90077-1851
310/471-8066 • FAX 310/471-4969

Printed in the United States of America

Printed on recycled stock

Cover design by Heidi Frieder

Cover illustration by Brains

Library of Congress Cataloging in Publication Data

Joseph, Erik, 1959—

Glam scam: successfully avoiding the casting couch, and other talent and modeling scams / Erik Joseph

    p.   cm.

Includes bibliographical references and index.

ISBN 0-943728-66-5 (pbk.) : $13.95

1. Performing arts—Vocational guidance. 2. Models (Persons)—Vocational guidance. 3. Swindlers and swindling. I. Title.

PN1580.J63   1994

791'.023—dc20   94-16480

                                       CIP

FOREWORD

by
Linda Buzzell

Author of "How To Make It In Hollywood: and Director of the
Entertainment Industry Career Institute in Beverly Hills.

> *"This town loves a virgin."*
> *Anonymous Hollywood Agent*

Hollywood is like a vampire: always in search of new blood.

To maintain its perennial allure, the entertainment industry needs
regular infusions of irresistible new performing talent . . . just
out-of-film-school directing genius . . . fresh untold stories . . .
raw comic wackiness with a topical edge . . . and new "looks"
from unknown cinematographers. This ongoing talent search is
so important that the industry pays thousands of development
executives, casting directors and agents big bucks to search out
the next decade's stars in every category.

Unfortunately, as this book points out so well, that doesn't
mean there are jobs for all the wannabes or that everyone who
claims to be a legitimate Hollywood "talent scout" is the real
thing. And even the genuine producers, directors, executives and
agents can turn out to be wolves in Armani jackets!

Erik Joseph has done you—and the whole industry—a tremendous favor by writing GLAM SCAM. Listen to him very carefully! His advice could save your life or your career! Don't get
tricked, trapped or trashed by the wolves, vampires, sharks, or

coyotes in the Hollywood jungle. When a promise sounds too good to be true, it probably is.

If you choose show business as your career, take the time to get properly trained at legitimate school and listen carefully to your teacher's and fellow student's savvy tips. Read everything you can about what getting a job in America's highly competitive number two export industry really requires. This is a world-class business and the best talents in every category from every country want to get in on the action. You'd better be a world-class talent to take us on! And you need to develop world-class smarts and Rhino Skin to survive the Darwinian struggle for Hollywood success. The meek and naive don't last long here . . .

If, after reading this book and doing some serious soul searching, you decide Hollywood isn't for you, don't feel bad about giving this tough business a pass. Practice your art on a local or state level. Relax and enjoy a more normal and less stressful existence than we can offer you. Feel good that you earn a steady paycheck and savor a peaceful family life while your showbiz colleagues are sweating the callbacks and the rent check.

But if you decide to go for it, get ready for a wild ride. One thing I can promise you: Hollywood is never boring. Sometimes a grind, sure. Ruthless, frequently. Even brutal, every once in a while. But the industry will present you with the kinds of challenge that people who thrive on risk-taking, action and competition adore. If you're smart, talented, well-prepared, persistent—and do your schmoozing—you may be one of the lucky people who gets to do The Wild Thing in Tinseltown.

Just don't let those Glam Scams slow you down.

ACKNOWLEDGMENTS

This reference book was made possible with the assistance of various industry-related resources.

Thanks to: Pamela Ackerman, Dawn Allen, The Arthur Company, The Association of Film Commissioners International, Wanda Baerga, Nina Blanchard, Fay Bordy, Polly Businger, Linda Buzzell, K. Callan, Gil Cofrancesco, Deke Castelman, Delores Chevron, Liz Christiansen, Bethany Coffey, The Council of Better Business Bureaus, Timothy B. Davis, Richard deBlois, Dramaline Publications, Dr. Linda Duree, Reed Farrell, Charles FitzSimons, Kelly Howard, Gerald Gordon, Michael Harrah, Dr. Edna Hermann, Robin Holabird, The Hollywood Chamber of Commerce, Mary Beth Horiai, David Horowitz, Barbara Thompson Howell, Debra Innes, The Las Vegas Metro Police Fraud Division, Larry Lee, Patikay Lee, Rosemary R. Lewis and M.K. Lewis, Dr. Carole Lieberman, Mark Locher, The Los Angeles Better Business Bureau, Karen Lustgarden, Jennifer Martie, Maria Martie, Joan Meyer, Chester L. Migden, Marilyn Morrison, Ted Mortarotti, The National Fraud Center, Marilyn Newton, Lori Noble, Troy Perkins, Alecia Prentiss, Gerard W. Purcell, Tracy Reagan, Sam Riddle, Dr. Elaine Rodino, Barbara Elman Schiffman, Seven Arts Press, Janet Spiegel, Neil K. Spotts, Ira David Sternberg, Donna Tanner, Laurie Thompson, Mike Walker, Janice Weideman, Elmarie Wendel, Roger Young, Lee Zaichick. Much appreciation to: Bob Hirsch, Candace Morrison, Joan Singleton and Bethann Wetzel.

Special thanks to my brother, Kurt, and my parents, June and Art.

TALENT & MODELS
RED FLAG CHECKLIST

The following cautions are designed to keep talent and models safe:

✔ **Be suspicious!** There are no guarantees—or guaranteed jobs—in the entertainment industry.

✔ **Listen to your instincts.** They could save your life as you follow your dreams.

✔ **Know the talent agency laws in your area** (city, county, state).

✔ **Use a licensed talent agency.**

✔ **Stay away from talent agents who want up-front employment fees.** (This is against the law in most states.)

✔ **Check everything out before** you go to the interview.

✔ Have at least **two reputable consumer sources** of information.

✔ **Do not assume** want ads for actors or models are legitimate simply because they appear in a newspaper.

✔ **Beware of opportunities sounding too good to be true** (once in a lifetime, no experience required.) They usually are.

✔ **Never send or give money** to anyone who promises membership in a performer's union. Always check with the union first.

✔ **Never pay money in advance** for postage, advertising, registration, categorization or filing fees (an illegal practice in some states.)

✔ If you are unfamiliar with the agent, producer or photographer—**do not go on the interview alone!**

✔ **Do not interview in apartments or weekly rentals.**

✔ **If you are uncomfortable with an interview FOR ANY REASON, leave!** There will be other interviews, other jobs.

✔ **Read all releases and contracts carefully before signing them.**

TABLE OF CONTENTS

MONOLOGUE

From "Monologues They Haven't Heard":

DIANE. 18-25. Diane, a girl with dignity and self-respect, spurns the casting couch.

DIANE

Look, friend, let me give you a quick little history. Okay? I came out here from Dayton, Ohio two years ago. Hitched out, as a matter of fact, with a pervert in an RV. He tried to get me into the back of the thing for 2500 miles. He was sex on wheels, that guy, sex on wheels. But I didn't cave in. And I intend to keep it this way. I came out here to act, to make it with talent, if I have any. If I don't, back to Dayton and a job at GE.

I've heard all the angles out here. I've had every proposition from A to Z. And so far I've gotten by without becoming a tramp.

I may not be working right now, may not be "up for a series," but I'm also not up for you! Now or ever! If I make it, whatever the hell 'making it' is, and I'm beginning to wonder altogether, I'll make it on my feet, not on my back!

So, here's your script. Enjoy it. Frankly, I didn't. I really can't get into a twenty year old hooker who lays a heart patient in the back of an ambulance. I wouldn't make it in the back of an RV for free and I won't make it in the back of an ambulance for scale. See you 'round, Film Person.

INTRODUCTION

"There are a lot of teachers, photographers, managers and others who are ready to take actor's money."
K. Callan, actress/author (*LA Agent Book*)

What is a *glam scam* ? Anyone who claims to be a glamour industry insider for the purposes of unlawful, unethical or immoral personal gain, usually either financial or sexual in nature.

Glam scams are perpetrated by fakes, pretenders, lawbreakers and law-benders, fly-by-nighters, crooks, perverts, sociopaths, even psychopaths. What they want to do to you, they have already done to someone else. Who are the targets? Based on cases and complaints over nearly ten years, primary targets are **females** (13-35 years old), **parents** and **young men**. From Texas to Michigan, Toronto to New South Wales, Alaska, San Diego and Portland—glam scams occur everywhere and anywhere, at anytime. Some have even swept across the U.S. and back!

Ever since Lana Turner was "discovered" on a drugstore stool, scam artists pretending to be bigtime agents and producers have approached women at malls, movie theaters, libraries, health clubs, campuses, the beach, public parks, restaurants, everywhere. The myth has been exploited to harmful proportions. No one is immune to promises of stardom made by a Hollywood "agent", "producer", "fashion photographer" or "casting director." Certainly many *dream makers* are legitimate. But some are actually *dream parasites* , whose purpose is to rob, exploit, even hurt.

Times have changed. The reality is, the days of "I can make you a star!" are gone. Rapists have claimed to be photographers, kidnappers have posed as producers, murderers have pretended to be agents. Recent magazine articles—People, Premiere, *Film Threat, Sassy, Glamour*—and television shows—*Dateline: NBC* , *Geraldo, Joan Rivers, FBI: The Untold Stories, Steals & Deals, Shame On You, Jenny Jones, 48 Hours, Inside Edition, Jane Whitney, Jerry Springer, Montel Williams*—have devoted reports to glam scams. An award-winning play, which was later made into a motion picture, ("Six Degrees of Separation") was written about a famous entertainment industry-related scam. Because it happens every day and not just in Hollywood!

Forget about being discovered at Schwab's pharmacy or in front of Mann's Chinese Theater. Pay no attention to that magazine advertisement that says anybody can be a movie star. Ignore that classified ad in your local newspaper that promises "$$$" and travel as a "Hostess" in the Orient. Forget about starmaker kits and "chance of a lifetime" opportunities. Investigate the business card of that photographer or agent who approached you at that club. The mechanisms of the star-making machinery do not include people who hang out at the local mall looking for undiscovered talent. The entertainment industry is no longer that simple.

ILLEGAL VS UNETHICAL
Illegal: against the law.
Unethical: against the rules.

Glam scams are illegal, unethical (or immoral) or all the above. The action against an illegal operation involves enforcement proceedings. Recourse against an unethical business operation can be less official. Crimes against nature, society or people are easier to prove and punish than are dishonesty, impropriety or misconduct. Illegal involves disregard for law; unethical implicates wrongful conduct. A determination must be made concerning *illegal* or *unethical* . How wrong is it?

A general rule of thumb to apply is that any individual or business involved in the exchange of money or goods or services must posses a business license. Nearly all forms of commerce are regulated and enforced.

SCAM vs COME-ON
> *Scam*: the plan to defraud.
> *Come-on*: the lure.

People are heard to say, "It's not really a scam, it's more of a...come-on." Scams can humiliate and hurt. Come-ons leave us feeling foolish. Scams induce public outcry. Come-ons victimize on a more personal level. The difference between a scam and a come-on is the difference between:*"They must be stopped!"* and *"Someone should do something about that."*

Whether it is illegal or unethical, a scam or a come-on— all cause harm. More importantly, *all are preventable!*

Do not abandon your dreams of being an actor, model or entertainer. But realize that there is no easy way. Be ambitious, yet suspicious. And be cautious and prepared, never desperate.

Throughout this book, you will notice *"RED FLAG ALERT"* reminders. At the very end of this book, there is a *RED FLAG ALERT* checklist. . . refer to it often.

✔   *RED FLAG ALERT*: **There are no guarantees in the entertainment industry.**

Why are there so many glam scams? Because laws and policies are inconsistent, from state-to-state, county-to-county, city-to-city and from newspaper-to-newspaper. Glam scam operators thrive on this confusion. It's not surprising that the most convenient plea by glam scammers is ignorance of the law. **Ignorance of the law is no excuse!** Glam scam operators also tell us what we want—*what we need* —to hear: *"You have what it takes, it's easy..."*

There are excellent books available that tell you how to make it as an actor or model, but it is usually wiser to know what *not to do* first, before you *do* . It is up to you—actors, actresses, models, performers and **parents**! Don't get caught in a *glam scam*. This book is a guide, a reference, a business tool. It was written to keep you safe because you are on your own.

Most importantly...

✔ Be pro-active!

✔ Be prepared and aware.

✔ Listen to your instincts as you follow your dreams.

Erik Joseph

1

IT CAN HAPPEN TO YOU!

"I can make you a star!"—**Classic glam scam line**

The following incidents are true. Names of victims have been withheld as a consideration to friends and families. This is the tip of the iceberg . . .

April 1, 1984: On a typically warm and windy Sunday in a small town in a southwestern state, a straight 'A' high school student entered her first modeling contest. It was a popular magazine cover search held at a local mall. She was nervous, so she went alone. But what could be safer? There would be a large crowd watching the prestigious competition in the largest shopping mall in town, in the middle of the afternoon! At four o'clock, she was seen leaving the mall with Christopher Bernard Wilder. This town was just another stop for Wilder on his 47 day 8,000 mile cross-country sadomasochistic murder spree. The young woman never had a chance. She became a Wilder victim.

Christopher Wilder found his victims in shopping malls. He introduced himself as a fashion photographer or modeling agent. His trail of terror, torture, rape and murder included victims in **Oklahoma, Nevada, Colorado, Texas, California, Indiana, Florida** and **New York**. He eventually became the FBI's most wanted fugitive. An FBI official called the search for Wilder the agency's "most extensive fugitive manhunt" ever. At one time or another, the FBI had more than half their agents looking for Wilder.

By all accounts, the young woman in the small town was an unlikely victim. She was part of a strong, loving family. She had the respect of her teachers, and the admiration of her friends. She was considered to be levelheaded and only entered the contest to try something different.

Newspaper accounts described her this way: *"No one who met her failed to come away with the impression that she was a winner. [She] was simply too bright, ambitious and involved, not to make a difference during her life."*

Thirty-nine year-old Christopher Bernard Wilder was a spellbinding millionaire. At the time, he was free on bail pending the trial for the kidnapping-assault of two teenage girls in Sydney, Australia. He used various aliases and took on different appearances. Wilder was ultimately held responsible for the murders and disappearances of 11 women. Authorities described Wilder as a twisted figure who preyed on fresh-faced young women at shopping malls, luring them with promises of modeling glamour and ultimately kidnapped, raped, tortured and eventually murdered them. In "Beauty Queen Killer," author Bruce Gibney wrote about Wilder: "Beauty queens, models and cheerleaders were his targets, all ambitious and all vulnerable to this millionaire-loner's seductive but deadly charms."

Police officers eventually cornered Wilder in Colebrook, New Hampshire. Instead of surrendering, Christopher Bernard Wilder struggled with a police officer. Some reports say Wilder's own gun discharged into his chest during the fight; other reports say Wilder committed suicide by aiming for his heart.

In 1987, The Portland Oregonian refused to run a classified advertisement placed by Christopher David Star. The "want" ad was looking for actors for a movie.

April 10, 1992: The *Portland Oregonian* published a classified ad seeking actors for a movie called, "I Am A Special Agent".

The Oregon film commission reported no knowledge of such a production.

April 23, 1992: The *Portland Oregonian* reported that police had arrested Christopher David Star, also known as Chad Cadrecha and several other aliases, ". . . on allegations of sex abuse involving a man who responded to a newspaper classified advertisement seeking actors for a movie."

The man was told by Star that he had to be photographed nude for a scene in the movie. Star reportedly fondled the man's genitals without consent during the photo session.

May 18, 1987, South Lake Tahoe, California: FBI officials stormed Herbert J. Coddington's rented mobile home and rescued two teenage girls. Also inside, were the strangled bodies of two older women stuffed in garbage bags. Coddington had kidnapped the foursome two days earlier...

A week before the kidnapping, "Mark Clayton" (Coddington) posed as a producer of an antidrug video and canvassed Reno talent and modeling agencies. He was seeking "All-American" girls between the ages of 12 and 18. One talent agent would later describe "Clayton" as looking like he hadn't taken a bath in weeks. She added that he also appeared very nervous, even his hands were sweaty and shaky. "Clayton" also did not present a business card. Another agent said "Clayton" wouldn't look her in the eye. "Clayton" chose two aspiring models, ages 12 and 14 and arranged a photo session with their agent.

May 16: The 68 year-old agent and her 72 year-old friend drove the two girls to a shopping mall parking lot, where they met "Clayton". They took his car and he drove the group to his secluded South Lake Tahoe mobile home. Once there, "Clayton" strangled the two women to death. He held the two girls captive in a soundproof room for two and a half days.

May 18: FBI agents busted into Coddington's mobile home and apprehended Coddington. Later, Coddington would detail his elaborate plan to murder the two girls in view of news cameras.

July 8, Placerville, California: Coddington pleaded innocent and innocent by reason of insanity to multiple charges of kidnapping, murder and sexual assault. Prosecutors asked for the death penalty.

July 22: Coddington was charged with the unrelated 1981 abduction, rape and strangulation of a 12 year-old Las Vegas girl.

Herbert J. Coddington is currently serving two life sentences, plus thirty-two years.

★

September 19, 1987, Bullhead City, Arizona: A seventeen year old girl was found floating in the Colorado River. Arizona authorities determined she died of strangulation. She had been missing for eight days.

April 29, 1992: Las Vegas police obtained an arrest warrant for 52 year old Thomas Preston, in connection with the young woman's murder. Police said Preston told her he was a talent agent who could develop a modeling career for her.

Preston is last heard of living and working in **Anacortes, Washington.**

April 30, 1992: Preston was arrested in **South Dakota** and charged with murder.

★

December 8, 1988, Las Vegas, Nevada: Max Carson, a self-proclaimed movie producer was forced to close his office by state licensing authorities for operating without proper business licenses and permits.

February 28, 1992: The *Hollywood Reporter* headline read, "Rape Suspect Tells Victims He's Producer." The article reported that William John Wood, a.k.a. Max Carson, faced state and federal criminal charges "of kidnapping, sexual assault and battery of an aspiring Las Vegas model who was allegedly lured to a motel room to prepare for a commercial [Carson was producing]."

Wood is a suspected serial rapist who poses as a **Hollywood** producer, talent agent or owner of a modeling studio. He is currently sought as a fugitive by the FBI.

February 20, 1989, Henderson, Nevada: Robert Love/Love Management placed a classified ad representing himself as a talent agent and manager. The ad mentioned a $150 fee. The fee involved a photo and makeup session at his temporary business address—his apartment.

June 27, 1991: A *Las Vegas Sun* headline reported "Police Hunt Porn Suspect." *"A man faced criminal charges for taking nude photos of a 17 year old girl . . .*

"Robert Gruber, who also uses the name Bob Love was released from the Clark County Detention Center on $12,000 bail . . . Detectives had gone to [Gruber's] apartment to investigate complaints from women who had applied for a receptionist's job. Police said he had listed the job in classified newspaper advertisements.

The women told police Gruber said they could make more money modeling lingerie or by posing in the nude. He would attempt to convince them to pose for photographs police said."

April 13, 1991, San Diego, California: A "producer" from Paramount Pictures called a licensed talent agency. He needed 20 athletic men for a baseball movie, starring Kevin Bacon. Filming would start in a couple of days at Jack Murphy Stadium, so the "producer" needed local talent fast! The producer told the agency, "Some of the actors may get lines so all 20 need to mail $250 for SAG initiation dues."

The agency called Paramount Pictures and asked about the film. Paramount had no knowledge of such a project. The agency reported the incident to the authorities.

June 28, 1992, across the U.S: For nine months a scam using computerized telephone answering systems and electronic money transfer networks defrauded hundreds of actors nationwide. Using the names "Patrick Swayze Productions" or "Rob Lowe Productions," this glam scam hit **Chicago, Milwaukee, Phoenix, Las Vegas, Boise, Memphis, Toledo, Sacramento and San Diego**, offering actors parts in nonexistent movies and Screen Actors Guild membership cards through the mail for $250-$450.

Film Commissions and the Screen Actors Guild offices around the country issued warnings to actors not to send money to any production company for "union dues." No suspects were found.

December 11, 1992, Toronto, Ontario, Canada: Selva Kumar Subbiah, alias Richard Wild, plead guilty to 14 counts of sexual assault after posing as a talent scout, then drugging his victims before having sex with them. Subbiah also posed as a dancer with Michael Jackson's world tour and as a photographer. Police said he lured at least 25 women by promising them work as actresses or models.

October 8, 1992, Burbank, California: Wallace Kaye, a licensed and Screen Actors Guild franchised Hollywood talent agent, was arrested for alleged sexual attacks on six actresses and models, including an assault on an undercover police officer.

More actresses came forward and Kaye was eventually charged with 11 counts of sexual battery and false imprisonment.

June 9, 1993, Pasadena, California: Kaye was found guilty on nine counts and received a five-year four-month jail sentence and a $1500 fine.

During auditions, Kaye encouraged the aspiring actresses to improvise scenes of sexual seduction. He then pinned the actresses and fondled them. Kaye attempted to justify his actions, saying that improvising scenes of foreplay is a common talent agent function.

February 3, 1993, New York City, New York: "Dream Scheme," a segment on *"48 Hours"*, examined complaints against

U.S. Models, Inc. Perspective models told *"48 Hours"* they were lured by the following newspaper classified ad:

> *Models Actors & Kids*
> *For magazines, TV, fashion, movies.*
> *All ages, no experience. (212) 675-9150.*

U.S. Models would tell the aspiring models it was easy to get modeling jobs, but they needed photos. U.S. Models would then arrange photo sessions that ultimately cost the models hundreds of dollars. A *"48 Hours"* undercover reporter was told by a U.S. Models representative, "You can make money, lots..." The New York City Better Business Bureau said of U.S. Models' operation: "It's unethical, immoral and sometimes it is illegal."

"48 Hours" returned to U.S. Models, Inc. a few days later to find a vacant office.

June 17, 1993, Los Angeles, California: Three young, aspiring actresses claimed on *Jenny Jones* that they attended a residential acting program in Los Angeles and were sexually harassed. They said "The Program" was a dubious operation that included a casting couch and hidden charges.

"The Program's" $2750 cost was broken down this way: Rent for 11 weeks, $1800; two classes per week (at $450 per class), $900; registration, $50. A $500 nonrefundable deposit was required upon acceptance. (See State-by-State/Ohio section, Sample ads: "Actors/Audition. L.A. Opportunity . . .")

July 22, 1993, Detroit, Michigan: The *Detroit Free Press* reported that Marc Hendley, also known as "Angel," was sitting in the Wayne County Jail on multiple counts of fraud. As *"Angela* Barnett," Hendley became known as the "Transvestite Scam Artist" and the "Cross-dressing Con."

For over a year *she* scammed free limousines, airplane tickets, elaborate bouquets of flowers, hotel suits, Learjet flights, meals, expensive champagne, cellular phone service and more! How did *she* fool so many people from **Washington D.C.** to Detroit, **Las Vegas** and **Chicago**? Easy. Hendley claimed to be a movie star, a temperamental daytime drama actress named "Tricia Tucker," a studio executive, a hotel/casino executive, the executive's female secretary and a producer's assistant. *She* also claimed to be a frequent guest of daytime talk shows.

August 18, 1993, Las Vegas, Nevada: Marc Hendley is ordered held on $50,000 bail.

September 2, 1993: A Las Vegas District Judge sentences Hendley to six years in prison.

September 2, 1993: *The Hollywood Reporter* headline read "Ex-Agent Ordered to Pay Harassed Model $7,000." An attorney for the California Labor Commission stated in a report that former talent agent Kenneth Vrana threatened an actress with loss of employment referrals if she did not have sex with him.

The article went on to say that Vrana has formed Professional Management Development, a management company, that places ads in newspapers promising high paying jobs for actors and models. The California Department of Industrial Relations said that such practices are in violation of state law.

December 13, 1993: The classified ad on the following page appeared in *La Opinion*, Los Angeles' leading Spanish-language newspaper.

This company promised 200 "Extras" $120 a day, plus food, transportation and costumes. The only requirement was that applicants provide the company with headshot photos. The small print at the bottom of the ad, *"Cobramos $25 por portafolio de fotos"* translates to *"We charge $25 for photo portfolios."* Hollywood Hispanic Productions told the California Labor Commission that the company was a talent agency. If this were true, the company would have been in violation of state law, since California prohibits talent agencies from collecting photo fees. Fact was, Hol-

---

ATENCION EXTRAS DE CINE

Pelicula en filmacion solicita 200 personas con urgencia de todas edades para trabajar como publico por 2 semanas.

No necesita experiencia ni hablar ingles. $120 diarios mas comida, transportacion y yestuario.

CONTRATACION INMEDIATA

HOLLYWOOD HISPANIC PRO.
Cobramos $25 por portafolio de fotos.

---

lywood Hispanic Productions was not licensed as anything and was not involved in any known production!

January 17, 1993: *The Hollywood Reporter* published this Letter to The Editor from *La Opinion.*:

"You identified La Opinion *as having published a deceptive ad placed by a company called Hollywood Hispanic Productions. Since 1926, La Opinion has been committed to publishing a daily Spanish-language newspaper of the highest quality. Assuring the integrity of the advertising we accept for the publication is an essential part of achieving this aim.*

Our newspaper obtained copies of this company's fictitious business name statement, Talent Agency Bond and membership card from the Better Business Bureau. Unfortunately, not all of this documentation was valid.

La Opinion *regrets that our readers were subjected to such an unscrupulous business practice. We have reviewed our advertising acceptance policy regarding talent agencies to assure that this type of situation does not occur in the future."*

January 14, 1993, Norwalk, California: Tito David Valdez, Jr., a 23 year-old host of "Hollywood Haze"—a cable access program—was sentenced to 14 years in prison for raping a 13 year-old girl. Valdez lured the girl into his house with the promise of a job interview. Valdez, along with his father, also faces charges of hiring a hitman to kill the 13 year-old victim before she testified!

★

More cases than these are documented—from **Toronto, Canada,** to **Corpus Christy, Texas,** from **Daytona Beach, Florida** to **New South Wales, Australia.** Don't let it happen to *you* !

In each of these cases, the victims were lured into dangerous situations by the perpetrators' purposeful schemes. The glam scam operators' tools of the trade include the use of classified ads, business cards and various other "come-ons". Perhaps if these aspiring actors and models knew what *not to do,* they wouldn't have become undeserving victims of *glam scams* .

[Ed. Note—A few weeks prior to publication of The Glam Scam, Erik Joseph received a call from a concerned film office director. A "photographer from Hollywood" had approached "Alice," a 19 year old, at a hamburger stand. The "photographer" told "Alice" that she had the perfect look and he could make her a star, if she flew to Los Angeles with him—immediately! Excited about becoming rich and famous, "Alice" called her mother and said she was going. Feeling that something wasn't right, "Alice's" mother promptly phoned the police. The police advised her to check out the photographer with the film office.

Now very worried and flustered, "Alice's" mother left a nonworking phone number with the office's secretary. With the obvious red flags revealing a potentially dangerous situation, the film office called Erik for recommendations. The agreed upon plan was to somehow forestall "Alice" until at least more information could be obtained on the "photographer."

Erik told the film office to find out which flights departed for Los Angeles in the next hour. There was only one flight. An "important message" was was then left at the check-in counter for "Alice" to call her mother. Also, for the ensuing two hours the "photographer" was paged in hopes of engaging him in a conversation that would reveal more about his plans and/or background. Airport security was also notified.

"Alice" was from an economically depressed area of her city. In her brief and fitful conversation with the film office secretary, "Alice's" mother revealed that her daughter "desperately wanted out. . ."

Nothing was ever heard of "Alice" again.]

2

CLASSIFIED ADS

"GET DISCOVERED! Need children & adults of all ages, sizes, nationalities for film/tv. Earn up to $6,000." —newspaper classified ad

A model called on the following classified ad . . .

> ### HOSTESSES
> Chance of a lifetime, needed to work in Orient. Ages 21-32. Round Trip ticket guaranteed. $500 cash on arrival. Airline ticket held in your posession.
> Call for details. 252-0820

Her brief phone conversation with the company went like this:

> Model: *Hi, I'm calling about the ad in the paper.*
> Company: That position has been filled.
> Model: *You only had one position?*
> Company: All positions have been filled.
> Model: *What were they for?*
> Company: I don't know.
> Model: *Well, what's the name of the company?*
> Company: (Click.)

Sound like a legitimate company?

★

If an ad instructs you to call between certain hours, call *before* or *after* the specified times and notice how the phone is answered. Is it answered at all? Or, does someone drone *"This is Arnie..."* Professional entertainment industry companies realize show business is a nonstop business, so they use answering machines with off-hours instructions.

THE TRADES

Perhaps you have seen ads that say: *"Hollywood Agents Want You! No Experience Necessary."* How about *"Get Discovered!"* or, *"Does Your Child Want To Be A Star? No fee."* Advertisements for talent or models in entertainment publications, fan magazines and teen magazines are sales pitches for products, classes or costly phone services. Better Business Bureaus warn not to be taken in by these types of ads.

Industry trade publications, such as the **Hollywood Reporter, Daily Variety**, **Drama-logue** and **Back Stage**, publish ads (i.e., casting calls, audition notices) for talent and models. A small ad in an industry trade publication can cost as little as $50. The *Hollywood Reporter, Daily Variety*, *Drama-logue* and *Back Stage and BackStage/West* each has policies dictating classified advertising. Editors of these publications do their best to detect unscrupulous job offers, come-ons for products or services and suspicious casting calls. Still, some glam scams continue to elude their efforts.

The *Hollywood Reporter* does not publish a disclaimer. If a problem occurs with a talent call or modeling related ad, the *Hollywood Reporter* will investigate the complaint. "We're concerned about anything that could be hurtful to talent," says Classified Advertising Manager Liz Christensen. The ad must contain a statement of applicable fees.

Disclaimers which assume "no responsibility to any party for the content of the classified advertisement," are periodically published in the classified section of *Daily Variety*. According to *Daily Variety*, most talent and model calls come from familiar sources, such as major production companies or studios. Ads run by studios usually have the studio's logo in the ad. "Audition" ads are only accepted from domestic companies and all fees must be specified in the ad. Vague ads are not accepted. Ads that seem suspicious are not accepted. *Daily Variety* will not knowingly run ads for photo come-ons or escort services. Serious complaints are forwarded to the police department, Better Business Bureau and other industry trade publications.

Drama-logue prints disclaimers. *Drama-logue's* disclaimers are changed, moved, highlighted, boxed and bolded, to be conspicuous. Drama-logue will only publish model calls from agencies licensed in the state of California. *Drama-logue* checks out their ads before they print them and will not run ads that do not appear to be legitimate. Co-publisher and Editor-in-Chief, Fay Bordy, says the magazine developed their classified ad criteria over 23 years of operation. Bordy has monitored *Drama-logue's* classified ads for over nine years. Her advice to talent and models is, "Don't be afraid to ask questions of individuals and companies. Yes and no answers are bad signs. You shouldn't have to pull teeth for information."

Back Stage and *Back Stage/West* lists casting/audition notices and paid advertising. Casting notices are closely scrutinized. Advertising Sales Director Scott Berg says Back Stage also requires that all advertising "be up front about any solicitations." Modeling agencies are requested to submit ads on company letterhead, accompanied by their license numbers. *Back Stage* will pull questionable ads, if complaints are received. *Back Stage* prints a conspicuous disclaimer.

Look for specifics in "Audition" ads. If the ad wants to reach as many people as possible, they are generally trying to sell something. Put your emotions aside and investigate the company that placed the ad.

Legitimate talent agencies do not rely on finding talent by placing newspaper classified ads. Answering classified ads in newspapers is **not** a good way to obtain valid acting or modeling jobs. Scam operators are always looking for ways to cut corners and a newspaper classified ad is an inexpensive, easy way to reach the general public.

✔ *RED FLAG ALERT* : **The secret to reading classified ads soliciting talent and models is to not let them lead you on. They want you to read between the lines, because that's where it says, "***I can make you a star!***"**

Take a look at this actual newspaper classified ad. Can you spot the danger signs?

MODELS WANTED.
No Experience Necessary!

This is a chance of a lifetime to be featured in a soon to be published and nationally marketed, high-quality swimsuit calendar, with the chance to be featured in your own nationally marketed poster. We are looking for: 1) Coeds or girls who will be attending college within the next two years; 2) Also, women who have what it takes to be a Calendar Girl. Send photos, *personal info and $10 processing fee.*

There are several *red flags* in this glamorous-looking offer:

1. "No Experience Necessary" and "Chance of a Lifetime" are tried and true come-on lines.
2. The company is unnamed.
3. They request personal information.
4. They want money up front.
5. They are operating through the mail.

6.   They are soliciting *"girls who will be attending college within the next two years"* —16 and 17 year olds!

SAMPLE ADS

Here are other ads sampled from entertainment magazines, fan magazines, teen magazines, newspapers and industry trade publications across the U.S. and Canada. These are actual ads. Read them closely and determine if you would respond.

"Modeling. . . Treat yourself tonight. Outcall only."
(An out-call service advertising in a newspaper classified ad section under "Models".)

"Models. . . Attention: Spokespeople wanted for surf wear. Models chosen will be involved in media blitz, print work, and promotions. Apply at hotel pool area between 12—5 PM. Do not call hotel."
(Meeting at hotel pools or restaurants is not advised unless conducted under the authority of a major film or television studio or recognizable production company. Even then, take a friend.)

"Celebrity look-a-likes, dancers and comics wanted for new resort production show."
(Call the resort to see what they know about the production.)

"Get into S.A.G.! Get your S.A.G. card quickly and easily. . . Guaranteed!"
(If they are offering to sell Screen Actors Guild cards, they are not legitimate and may be breaking the law.)

"Models Wanted! Hottest young guys for calendars, posters, and more! No experience necessary, Ages 15-23 only. National exposure, strictly legit! "
(Is this an agency? Management company? Photographer? Or . . ? *"No experience necessary"* is a red flag. The solicitation for underage models is a serious concern.)

"Models—Gorgeous females wanted for Playboy *magazine."*
(This is not the way *Playboy* finds its centerfolds.)

Advertisement which appeared in the Los Angeles Times.

"Casting Actresses. . . young, inexperienced, big-breasted women, not bashful, and willing to learn, for horror film."

(They probably don't even have film in the camera!)

"Models—kids, ages 1-16 to model clothes for catalogs, fashion ads, TV commercials, and movies."

(Your local film commission or a licensed talent agency will probably have more information about these "commercials, and movies.")

"Models. . . New magazine is looking for all females interested in modeling and acting. Guaranteed exposure and results!"

(No one can guarantee talent or models results!)

"Models. . . Talent Agency is seeking new faces for acting and modeling contracts. License #00001. Call now!

(Just because an agency lists a license number, does not mean they are licensed to do business in your city, county, or state. See Recourse section.)

"Radio/TV. . .your voice can earn you cash! Supplement your income."

(This company probably wants someone to sell vitamins, magazines, raffle tickets, etc. It could also be a phone sex line.)

"Models—Men 19-24, for figure photography publications. Photo I.D. required, $75./hr."

(There is no misleading information in this ad.)

Ignore ads from out-of-state companies for these reasons:
1. You forfeit the element of personal contact.
2. It will cost you money for long distance phone calls.
3. Photos sent through the mail can be damaged or lost.
4. Filing a long distance complaint is usually a lost cause.

Do not necessarily be impressed by license numbers and/ or out-of-state Chamber of Commerce memberships. A plaque on a wall does not automatically legitimize someone.

Not all casting notices are glam scams. On the previous page is a casting notice of a different sort that appeared in the

Los Angeles Times , June 28, 1992. Though the contest is over, the advertisement still makes you want to buy the book.

Casting call ads require careful analysis. For instance, if an ad said a company was holding an open casting call for 7-11 year old girls beyond their years, no experience necessary with interviews to be held on Saturday, you should be alarmed. Such an ad appeared in the *Hollywood Reporter* . Closer inspection revealed the title of the motion picture ("Interview With A Vampire"), the distribution company (Warner Bros.), the director's name (Neil Jordan), the producing company (Geffen Pictures) and the producer (Stephen Woolley). Needless to say, this was a legitimate casting call.

> ✔ *RED FLAG ALERT* : **If you see an ad that seems suspicious, call the proper licensing authorities and the police, and call or write the publication in which the ad appeared.**

CHECKLIST

If you feel you must respond to what seems to be a legitimate casting call in the classifieds, check this list first:

- ✔ Is the ad from an out-of-state company?

- ✔ Is it a "Chance of a lifetime opportunity" or require no experience?

- ✔ Do they request personal information?

- ✔ Are you required to pay first?

- ✔ Are they licensed to do business in your city, county and/or state?

- ✔ Is the "Suite Number" actually a Post Office Box?

3

BUSINESS CARDS

"And above all . . . don't need the work."
(Lewis & Lewis, "Your Film Acting Career")

A business card reveals a great deal of information. A business card is a fingerprint, a piece of tangible evidence, which may reflect the professionalism and intention of the person who offers it. Business cards can lend credibility or help expose a fraud. Does this mean you will be able to tell the good guys from the bad guys just by looking at a business card? Not always.

Examine business cards carefully. Consider how and where it was presented, the source, paper stock, printing and the message (i.e., names, titles, phrases, phone numbers, etc.). Look for union affiliations, professional organization and/or association logos printed on the card. Then call the union or association to check out the individual's credits and membership standing. Business cards are usually designed to tell you what you need to know about the card giver at a glance.

Here are some things to check:

✔ they talk about who they are and what they can do for you, but they don't have business cards.

✔ crumpled or dirty cards.

✔ paper-thin cards which have obviously been printed by a "dot-matrix" printer.

✔ overly busy cards (e.g., company name, description of service offered, artwork, a pitch for business, address and at least two phone numbers, other office locations—color graphics, bold letters, fancy fonts—all on one card!)

✔ the person lists two job descriptions which conflict or are not related (e.g., movie producer/dentist; fashion photographer/fitness trainer; talent manager/video sales, etc.)

✔ meaningless titles and pretentious phrases, such as: "Feature Entertainment Specialist"... "Video & Magazine stars!"... "Booking Director"... "Video Casting Rep".. "International Talent Scout", "Talent Screening Company", etc.

✔ cards with no address and/or phone number.

✔ cards with information scratched out or handwritten on the back.

✔ tacky cards (e.g., "models—dancers—actor/resses")

✔ cards with misspellings (e.g., "Calender Girls", "actressess", "filmaker", etc.)

✔ cards with only a toll free 800 number.

✔ cards presented by modeling or charm school directors who claim to be "International Scouts". (What are they scouting? Paying students, of course!)

✔ cards presented by an individual who claims to represent a company, yet there is no company name on the card.

✔ cards heavy on cutesy graphics (e.g., Richard $mith, Δrt Rocket, fatima CastinG, etc.)

✔ cards with three different contact names, each with a different phone number.

✔ a "producer", "agent", or "fashion photographer" whose business card reveals what they really do for a living—sales, writer, hairstylist, etc.

✔ cards that have blank spaces for anyone to fill in their name. For example:

```
THE TALENT PEOPLE, LTD.
_____
(fill in the blank)
Casting Director
                 555-8899
```

There are now self-serve machines in discount department stores and pizza parlors that will make personalized business cards within minutes. Just because someone presents you with his business card, does not mean you are obligated to give them any personal information.

✔ *RED FLAG ALERT:* **Do not give out personal information!**

A glam scam agent, producer or photographer may argue their point this way:

> We discover talent—fresh, new faces—by handing out
> our business cards and holding general interviews.
> That's how many bigtime actors and models were
> discovered."

...that's also exactly how 11 women were "discovered" by one of the most heinous glam scam offenders ever, Christopher Wilder (*see Chapter One, "It Can Happen To You!"*).

CHECKLIST

Here are three fictional business cards. Can you determine what is unprofessional about each? The answers follow:

```
  "Models" "Shows" "Stars"
  THE ENTERTAINMENT COMPANY
Vegas—Hollywood—Thunder Bay—Amsterdamn


Kay, Agent/Ventriloquist    "Bucky", Talent Mgr.
555-2221                            555-1117
```

This pretentious card is trying to impress you with fancy fonts and exotic office locations, yet nothing matches. Is "Vegas" Las Vegas? Do you really want to be represented by "Kay *whoever* ", an agent who talks out of both sides of her mouth and "Bucky *whoever*", the "Talent Mgr."? What does this company do?

```
D. SKAMMER, Jr.
Producer


                        P.O. Box 4
                        Los Angeles, CA
```

Beware of cards with P.O. Box addresses but no phone number. Doesn't this producer know his zip code? Remember, anyone can call himself a "producer."

```
┌─────────────────────────────────────┐
│                                       │
│                                       │
│            SUN DOG PRODS.             │
│             800-555-9988              │
│                                       │
│                                       │
└─────────────────────────────────────┘
```

Beware of cards with phone numbers only! Where is this company located and why do they want to keep it a secret?

4

COME-ONS

"If they've got it on film, you'd better watch out."—Actress Sharon Stone, "CBS This Morning"

Maybe that "talent company" really can help you get into movies . . . Maybe that person really is Madonna's tour manager. . . Maybe a producer in Bangkok is casting the next international blockbuster and you would be perfect in a supporting role . . . Maybe your daughter can be the next Papaya Queen . . . Maybe dancing topless in a Las Vegas revue would be fun . . .

Don't be fooled. Like the old saying goes: **If it sounds too good to be true, it probably is!** And you'll end up giving up more than you'll get.

Come-ons are enticements or inducements that usually are not illegal, but it follows that *you'll give up more than you'll get* Here's how to avoid some typical glam scam come-ons . . .

STARMAKER KITS

You may have spotted this type of ad in a tabloid or any free entertainment industry newspaper:

> *"Be on television! Many needed for commercials.*
> *Hiring all ages. Call for casting information in your area."*

They call themselves "talent companies." What these hard-sell, mail order businesses generally offer for $35-$125 is general information, common sense advice and a list of talent agencies across the country. They *guarantee* you will get work in films or television if you follow their instructions to the letter. If in three months you have not landed a television commercial, you may ask for a refund.

There are fundamental problems with these kinds of services. The agency lists they supply are almost always incomplete and often include agencies that are no longer in business. Any hope for a refund requires that you fill out a "refund form." Your refund may take four weeks to be processed. Question: *Where do you think these companies will be weeks—months—from now?*

Why pay for this information when you can receive better advice and current agency lists from your city, county, or state film commission? Also, all you need is accurate local information. If you live and work in Florida, a name and address of an agency in Oregon is practically useless.

Buyer beware.

PHOTO DIRECTORIES

Photo directories can be "headsheet" posters containing a few dozen photos or a book of hundreds of actor's and/or model's headshots or action photos. Talent almost always is required to pay to have their photograph/s included in photo directories. The usefulness of such a marketing strategy is questionable and costs can be staggering.

On May 12, 1992, *Dateline: NBC* aired a report on a photo directory called "Faces International." The segment was titled "Fantasies of Fame" and analyzed the practicality of "Faces'" quarterly directory in the industry. The *Dateline: NBC* report began: *"A lot of people have been told, it's just as easy as getting your picture in a magazine. A lot of people have been taken for a lot of money. . . "*

Dateline: NBC reporter, Michelle Gillen, posed, *"At some point, who hasn't wished for that elusive big break that would make all the difference?"* Gillen reported that "Faces" markets stardom for a price, promising a shortcut to casting directors looking for new talent. "Faces often delivers little more than disappointment," she concluded.

The report cited "Faces'" sales pitches to potential clients. Typical lines such as, "Your daughter needs to get on television," and "That's the cutest child I've ever seen," were reported come-on lines used by "Faces" sales representatives.

A *Dateline: NBC* hidden camera showed a "Faces" representative explain the process this way: "Faces" gives you an opportunity to get your face seen, so . . . "you'll be approached by a union. . . you'll be approached by an agent. . . then your career takes off!"

The cost of placing your photo in the "Faces" photo directory ranges from $95 for a small black and white passport size photo to $5,500 for a full page in color near the front of the book. A cover can cost $10,000.

Gillen also reported that not only does talent have to pay for placement in the "Faces" photo directory, but for the required photo session.

Does it work?

In the report, a former "Faces" photographer said he thinks "Faces" is a *"huge scam."*

Gillen asked a group of professional casting directors and agents if they knew of anyone in the entertainment industry who used "Faces" to find talent. The unanimous answer was, *"No!"* One agent said that a picture in a photo directory like "Faces" will not get you discovered. Gillen added that *Dateline: NBC "could find no reputable casting directors anywhere that used 'Faces' magazine to find talent."*

Are photo directories like "Faces International" legal? If they have a proper business license, they can operate. The *Dateline: NBC* report pointed out that the "Faces'" contract says "Faces" does not guarantee employment.

Again, buyer beware.

IMPOSTORS

Everyone enjoys meeting celebrities. Sometimes celebrities seem to be everywhere . . .

A man dressed as a "soap opera actress" chartered a private jet from Las Vegas to Chicago. While in Chicago, this impostor booked *herself* into an expensive hotel room, complete with limousine service. *She* paid for nothing because everyone believed *she* was a famous television star.

The *Miami Herald* reported that a woman was sentenced to six months in prison and a $500 fine for advertising that Chuck Norris would appear at a martial arts tournament that she was promoting. Instead of Norris, the woman hired an impersonator.

From the ridiculous to the sublime, celebrity impostors can show up anywhere at anytime! Impostors boldly pose as actors, rock stars, cousins of celebrities, managers of famous people, eminent producers and talent scouts. One or two quick and easy phone calls can expose them as frauds.

If you come across a "famous person" who personally asks for something free, verify who they are before you comply. Call the Screen Actors Guild (SAG) and ask for the "Agency" department. SAG will provide you with the "famous" actor or actresses' agent's phone number. Call the agent and ask if the person is, in fact, who they say they are. If no one is available to verify the celebrity's claim, get their autograph, preferably on a receipt. The receipt can serve as legal (and tax) evidence for services rendered. Then, follow up the next business day with phone calls to the SAG and/or the proper law enforcement authorities.

Keep in mind, impostors usually act alone.

TECHNO–CASTING

Techno-casting involves relatively new industry services: computers, modems, monitors, CD-Rom Drives, CD players, fax machines. In other words, access the Information Superhighway to transmit pictures and resumes of talent to studios, producers, casting directors, and advertising agencies! Techno-casting is designed to facilitate the casting process. Techno-casting can be a beneficial service for all involved, Or, for all the technology provided, utilizing techno-casting can be as futile as putting a video cassette in a toaster.

Cautiously evaluate the usefulness of techno-casting companies that charge talent yearly or monthly "on-line" or "processing" fees. Is what they offer the equivalent of a mass mailing? If so, save your money.

```
Name:                    Phone:
Address:
City:            State:   Zip:
Soc. Sec. No:                        YOUR
Age range:                          PICTURE
Sex: M/F       Nationality:  Race:    HERE
Height:  Weight:  Eyes:   Hair:
Agency:
Unions:
(Males) Shirt:        Pant:         Inseam:
         Shoes:       Hat:          Coat:
(Females) Dress:            Blouse:
   Shoe:       Hat:          Glove:
   Skirt:
Measurements:
Experience (films, television, commercials, music vid-
   eos, spokesperson, narration, etc.):
Training (theater, voice, dance, runway, etc.):
Languages:
Special talents:
```

Sample, standardized techno-casting resume

Preferably, submissions of pictures and resumes should be transmitted via FAX. Make sure your agent (or the techno-casting company) deletes all personal information (i.e., home phone/address, social security number) before initiating any transmissions.

Some techno-casting services require that the sender and receiver have compatible technology with specific monitors, high-speed modems, selected CD-disc drives or CD players. Some charge even more money for audio transfers, which requires the receiver to have a digital-to-audio sound board. In their slick brochures, hard-sell techno-casting companies target young talent, students and other performers with little or no experience. They *guarantee* they can put your picture and resume "on-line" to talent representatives worldwide. They claim techno-casting is *the wave of the future!*

Does it work? Some casting directors use techno-casting. On the other hand, one Los Angeles talent agent put it this way: "If you don't have the compatible technology, what good is it? Another opinion is that nobody in Hollywood has time to view endlessly scrolling computer screens looking for talent. Most importantly, evaluate the cost to you, the talent.

BEAUTY PAGEANTS

Beauty pageants are a multimillion dollar industry. They can offer fun, personal growth, social skills, and lifelong friendships. They should be fun and a learning experience. Enter pageants for your self, not for anyone else. At stake are titles, cash, crowns, tiaras, banners, robes, pins, sashes, plaques, trophies, travel, furs, cars, scholarships, jewelry, auditions, endorsement contracts and more.

There are thousands of pageants. Barbara Thompson Howell, author of "Tiara: An Insider's Guide to Choosing and Winning Pageants," writes that, "If you can honor it, harvest it, eat it, dig it up, celebrate it, or be proud of it, you can win a tiara in its name—whatever 'it' happens to be."

Many prominent and famous women were former pageant winners or queens for a day. Did you know that Sharon Stone was Miss Crawford County? Debbie Reynolds was Miss Burbank. "60 Minutes' "Diane Sawyer was America's Junior Miss. Paula Zahn was a former Illinois Teen Miss. Cybill Shepherd was Miss Teenage Memphis and won Miss Congeniality at the Miss Teenage America pageant. Oprah Winfrey was Miss Fire Prevention Beauty and later Miss Black Tennessee.

Most pageants are legitimately sanctioned or publicly endorsed events. There are many pageants that are neither. How do you know a good pageant from a bad pageant? There is no regulatory commission nor collective association which monitors the pageant industry. Once again, you are on your own.

✔ *RED FLAG ALERT:* **Inquire about the reputation of the pageant promoter.**

Mike Walker, President, Madison Square Garden Events, producers of the Miss USA, Miss Teen USA and Miss Universe pageants, says to take proper precautions. "Be careful and ask questions before becoming involved in beauty pageants. Is it a first-time event? Is the entry fee exorbitant? Where is it being held and how many contestants are allowed? Investigate the character and experience of the promoter. "

Ask questions, such as how long has the pageant been around? Is it sanctioned by a local, state, or national pageant organization? Perhaps the pageant emphasizes scholastic, social, community and extracurricular activities instead of beauty. Is the entry fee reasonable? What are the advertised or guaranteed prizes? Who are the judges? How will the competition be judged? What is the quality of the production and where will it be held? **Pageant consultant Troy Perkins** advises to "take the time to find out about the pageant; it could be a dream-maker or a dream-breaker."

How many winners will there be? The 1992 "Miss Glamour America Beauty and Talent Pageant" promised 90 winners. Perhaps it's good that they offered that many prizes, maybe it isn't. Ultimately, it depends on what you want out of a pageant.

What are the obligations of the winner? Is the winner expected to sign a contract? If so, what rights are granted or withheld as stipulated by the contract? Maybe the contract will limit modeling opportunities during your official reign.

In 1992, nine year old "Little Miss Georgia" was stripped of her crown because of a clause in her contract. The offense: she sang "Achy Breaky Heart" on consecutive days while representing two different crowns. On the other hand, national pageant organizers have been sued by winners for not providing promised prizes. It is also worth noting that pageant prizes, whatever form they take, may not be collectable until the duties of the "Queen" are fulfilled. In other words, at the end of her reign.

Make copies of all checks sent to pageant organizations. Retain receipts. Attend pageants before entering. Investigate. There are books, magazines, even newsletters devoted to the pageant industry.

Pageants can be expensive. *"Photo evaluation fees"* sometimes cost as much as $50; which doesn't necessarily qualify you for the pageant. Entry fees can range from $20—$1,000. And there may be numerous competitive categories within the pageant— "Best Smile", "Best Costume", "Best Talent", etc.— all costing extra to enter.

Other costs may include wardrobe, coaches, trainers, travel, accommodations, long distance phone calls, special talent lessons and possibly even corrective surgery.

Some pageants encourage contestants to sell raffle or admission tickets. Often there may be an award given for the most ticket sales. Yet, it should not be a shock if coincidentally the contestant who sells the most tickets is awarded the crown. THIS IS THE EXCEPTION, NOT THE RULE! Nonetheless, beware.

CONTESTS

Calendar Girl, hot legs, hot buns, teeny bikini, wet T-shirt, torn T-shirt, no T-shirt, naughty nightie, tight jeans, dirty-dancing-behind-the-sheets—there are thousands of nightclub and bar contests! Know this much: *many contests are fixed* . Bar owners and contest promoters use "shills," professional dancers whose entry fee is paid for, and are guaranteed to win. You, on the other hand, have paid to enter (or have been coerced by friends to enter) and have far and away "the best"—*whatever*—yet *have no chance of winning!*

Don't look to be "discovered" at one of these contests. In fact, police departments warn that bikini contests and pageants are hotbeds for glam scam operators.

MODEL SEARCHES

Some "model searches" are simply sales pitches for costly training programs, photography and makeup sessions, workshops and other products or services.

Find out about the reputation of the sponsor. Is it a cosmetic company? Is it an out-of-state talent agency? A chain of national photo studios? Perhaps they claim to be a "talent representational firm."

How much is the entry or admission fee? The photo and makeup session may be free, but entry fees may cost as much as

$750! And all payments may be nonrefundable and non-cancellable.

Read the fine print. Get details on the prizes. Okay, so winners receive airfare to New York City or Los Angeles—is it roundtrip? Are taxi fare and hotel accommodations included? How much is the "modeling scholarship" worth and what is the reputation of the "school?" Is the prize money in the form of cash, gift certificates or portfolio materials?

Are more details on the event available for free?

✔ *RED FLAG ALERT: Do not send any money until they provide you with more information.*

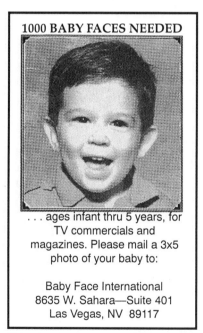

This advertisement appeared in a daily newspaper

The Elite Model Agency's 1993 "Look of the Year" search advertised "Over $700,000 in prizes," awarded by Elite. This contest's advertising tells you nearly all you need to know, including fine print explanations of the judges, judging procedure, Grand Prize, instructions on how to enter and a summary of the rules and winner's obligations. This international search is going on its tenth year and does not include a "photo evaluation fee". Complete official rules can be obtained by simply sending a self-addressed, stamped envelope to the sponsor.

Find out what you are entering. Analyze the promotion carefully. Is it a credible opportunity, or a come-on?

Do not mail personal information and/or photos of your child without knowing *who* you are sending it to! This company claimed to be "licensed". After being informed by the state film commission, Better Business Bureau and a few concerned parents that this company was not licensed in the state, county nor city, the newspaper excised the word "licensed" from the ad. And what type of business is this—a talent agency, production company, a photo directory? *"Suite 401"* was a post office box, not a business office.

Examine all opportunities thoroughly.

YELLOW PAGE LISTINGS

You have decided to try to break into acting or modeling. You have been told that it is best if you work through an agent, but you don't know how to find one. Why not start with the Yellow Pages? The Yellow Pages is a great place to find most things, from Acupuncturists to Zoos. However, the Yellow Pages **are not** necessarily the most reliable resource when it comes to finding reputable talent or modeling agencies in your area. Do not assume that just because an "agency" is listed in the Yellow Pages that the business is properly licensed.

Contact your local film commission or state, county or city licensing authorities for updated talent/modeling agency lists.

PERFORMING OVERSEAS

Job opportunities for entertainers and models exist all over the world. Ads for work overseas can be seen in newspapers located in cities nationwide:

```
┌─────────────────────────────────┐
│        FEMALES OVER 18!         │
│  Earn up to $5,000/week as an   │
│  Entertainer. Travel to Mexico, │
│  the Orient or Middle East.     │
└─────────────────────────────────┘
```

Some overseas job opportunities are legitimate; some involve escort services and sex clubs. Worst case scenarios have included imprisonment, forced prostitution, torture and disappearances.

Caution cannot be overly stressed in this area.

✔ *RED FLAG ALERT: When you are in a foreign country, you may have few rights, if any.*

When dealing with producers or agents hiring talent for jobs out of the United States, do not be satisfied with too-good-to-be-true offers. Dig deeper. Double-check references and reputations. Know *exactly* what you are getting into!

Producers must provide entertainers or models with a "work visa." Do not accept work in a foreign country with only a "tourist visa." You can be expelled and/or blacklisted by that country, if you are caught without the proper visa.

You will need a passport and a green card and a "work" (or "entertainment") visa.

A passport allows you to enter and leave the country. **Never surrender your passport to anyone for any reason!** If someone needs the information on your passport, provide a photocopy or write down what they require. Do not relinquish the passport itself.

Green cards (also called "alien cards") contain your passport information, your length of stay and purpose for being in the country. You apply for and receive your green card when you have arrived at your destination.

Visas permit certain activities. Visas are issued by the host country's embassy in the United States, before departure. There are various types of visas: tourist, work, student, etc. In Japan, entertainment work visas need to be renewed after three months and can be extended for a total of six months.

There are passport service companies that can deliver passports in twenty-four hours. The normal processing time for a passport and work visa is 3-4 weeks. Producers usually need performers to commit to the job 2-3 months ahead of the actual performance dates.

Before accepting an overseas job opportunity, ask numerous questions. What is your work schedule (hours a day; days a week; days off, etc.)? How much will you make and in what currency will you be paid? What is expected of the job?

✔ *RED FLAG ALERT*: **You can't lose a job by asking too many good questions.**

Will you be dancing? Singing? *Hostessing* ? An Escort? The contract should be very specific (and in English). Do not sign contracts written in a foreign language which you do not understand. Would you agree to a contract that contained the following statement?

私は有名になる為に何でもやります。

Signed: _____

If you cannot read and fully understand something, do not sign it.

Pay days are generally every 30 days and performers are usually paid in cash. Where and when will the show rehearse? Have you seen the costumes? Are you prepared to mend your own costumes? What is the concept of the show? Is the music ready? Rehearsals are typically held in the city where the producing company is based. Producers may provide transportation to rehearsals. Producers will pay for transportation from the rehearsal city to the show destination. Performers provide their own necessities (dance shoes, tights, makeup, etc.) Rehearsals should last 1 1/2-3 weeks. Ask if rehearsal pay is included in the contract.

What are the overseas accommodation arrangements? Who is paying for the room? What is the name of the hotel where you are performing? Where is it located? Will you be sharing a room? Will toiletries be available? Who will have keys to your hotel room besides you? Usually, only the front desk and security should have a duplicate key.

Are you expected to pay for your own meals or will you be provided with meal allowances?

What will the weather be like? What type of clothing should you take? Is there a dress code? Mary Beth Horiai, producer of Las Vegas revues for the **Las Vegas Show Biz** company, provides the following guidelines of things to bring when performing in Japan (also applicable to any overseas destination):

Guidelines When Performing in Japan (or Overseas)
1. Proper clothing according to the season. Always include a light jacket or coat.
2. Personal towels and pillows.
3. Battery operated alarm clock.
4. Translation dictionary.
5. Maps.
6. Books, music, video tapes.
7. Dance attire and accessories.
8. Umbrella and suntan oil.
9. Two or three outfits for special occasions.
10. Personal medicines.
11. Pictures of family and loved-ones.
12. Stationery, address book, envelopes, pens, pencils.
13. Preferred sugar substitutes and spices.

Horiai says, "white slavery, forced prostitution and illegal hostessing can happen if the entertainer has not properly investigated the job offer."

You need to know if telephones will be available. Overseas phone communication can be complicated. Know which public phones allow international calls. Be aware of time differences.

Establish an account with a phone company (MCI, SPRINT, AT&T) and travel with a calling card.

Is there a war on in the area? What areas of the city should be avoided? Are there special social or religious customs you should know about? For instance, in Japan, it is illegal for foreign visitors on entertainment visas to *"hostess." "Hostessing"* involves preparing and/or pouring drinks for customers. Performers are permitted to converse with customers, but are forbidden to pour drinks.

Ask the producer or agent for the U.S. Embassy and Consulate phone numbers. Do not expect an interpreter to be available on a twenty-four hour basis.

Teach friends or relatives how to say certain key phrases in the language of the country you will be visiting. They should at least be able to say the name of the hotel, your room number and phrases such as "Show Dancers" or "American members."

Keep your passport, green card and airline tickets in a safe place. Hotel safes are recommended.

The answers to most of these questions should be provided by the producer and/or in the written contract.

Ask if you have to do "consummation." Euphemistically speaking, this means *having sex with the customers* . If the agent will not answer this question—beware!

SHOWGIRLS

The three common misconceptions about "Showgirls" are: 1) all the dancers in the shows are nude; 2) you have to be very tall to be a dancer in a Las Vegas-style production show; 3) Showgirls are simply prancing mannequins.

There are various types of performers in production shows. "Principal dancers" usually dance in pairs ("adagio") and are not nude. "Covered dancers" are part of the chorus and are also not nude. "Specialty acts" can include acrobats, skaters, daredevils, magicians, etc., who rarely appear nude in the show. "Nude dancers" are part of the chorus and are topless. "Showgirls" are featured in production shows as covered and topless.

Showgirls are very tall and graceful and are trained dancers. All other dancers in production shows must be extremely talented and proportional in height and weight.

✔   *RED FLAG ALERT* : **Know what you are auditioning for!**

Legitimate production shows do not advertise in newspaper classified sections. Ads for open auditions usually appear in trade papers announcing the name of the production, specific requirements, venue (hotel/casino, cruise ship, etc.) and where and when the auditions will take place.

Auditions are usually held in a showroom, on stage, or at a reputable dance studio. **Do not audition for a production show in a hotel room or private residence.** Verify auditions with local dance teachers or other performers. Do not audition for a "nude" position in private. Legitimate dance auditions usually include the producer/s, choreographer and/or someone from the dance company.

Larry Lee, Director of Entertainment for the Tropicana Resort and Casino in Las Vegas and Producer of the FOLIES BERGERE, says the Folies show will not audition Showgirls or "Nude" dancers unless the co-producer, choreographer and/or show line captain are also present. He stresses that dressed dancers should not be required to reveal themselves if they are not auditioning for a "nude" dancing position. "Your figure can be seen without being nude," says Lee.

Inquire about auditions by calling the hotel and asking for the Entertainment Director. Or, ask the hotel operator for the backstage number. Try to speak with the show's line captain or company manager. If one of the performers answers, ask them a few brief questions. Most will be willing to share advice.

Performers in legitimate production shows should never be required, or asked, to do topless publicity. Be leery of producers who meet you, shower you with compliments, then immediately ask you out to dinner. Producers should not ask personal questions during auditions.

Beware if the producer wants to move fast. Production shows take tremendous planning. Be careful of productions which do not offer rehearsal pay.

There is no union or professional association with direct jurisdiction over dancers in production shows.

CHECKLIST

Starmaker kits
✔ Are they licensed to operate in your city?
✔ Can you get a free updated agency list from your local film commission?
✔ Do they guarantee you will get work in movies or television?

Photo directories
✔ Is the money better spent on other marketing strategies?
✔ Is it implied that all you need is for someone to see your photo—*and you'll be a star!*
✔ Do they require that you use their photographer?

Impostors
✔ Do they want something for free?
✔ Have you tried contacting their agent?

Techno- Casting
✔ Are they charging fees to talent?
✔ Is it the same as a mass-mailing of photos?
✔ Have you or your agent deleted all personal information from your resume?

Beauty Pageants
✔ Is the entry fee worth the crown?
✔ What is the pageant's history?
✔ Is the pageant sanctioned by a larger organization?

Contests
✔ Is it a fair competition?

Model Searches
✔ What is the reputation of the sponsor?
✔ Do they want an evaluation fee?
✔ Will they send more information for free?

Yellow Page listings
✔ Is the company properly licensed?

Performing Overseas
✔ What are the producer's credits?
✔ In what city is the producer's business license on file?
✔ Are you mature enough to adjust to different cultural conditions?
✔ Is "consummation" part of the job?

Showgirls
✔ Do you know what you are auditioning for?
✔ Is it a *private, closed-door* type of audition?
✔ Does the producer want to take topless photos of you for "publicity" purposes?

5

RELEASES

"I hereby grant you with my power-of-attorney and authorize you to collect and receive monies on my behalf and to deposit same in a checking account with any bank."

"I agree to be paid on a retroactive basis, when the investor makes the money available.."

Talent should never sign any contract containing either or both of these statements.

There are various types of legally binding entertainment industry Releases. Releases are abbreviated contracts designed to grant or withhold certain rights of the respective signing parties. Releases are legal agreements and authorizations. If you sign it, you agree to it! Talent and models should always retain reasonable control of their filmed, videotaped or photographed image. This is an area where agents and attorneys can serve talent best.

> ✔ *RED FLAG ALERT*: **Do not sign releases or contracts hastily or under pressure.**

Sometimes it may be better that you do not sign a particular release. You may not want to sign if . . .

- ✔ A photographer wants to sell and resell your photos.
- ✔ An agent wants half your wages.
- ✔ A personal manager asks you to sign away your legal rights.
- ✔ A casting director wants you to work for free.
- ✔ A producer requires that you pay to be in his movie.

Here is the basic agreement of a standard photo release used by many professional photographers:

> *In consideration for exposure, I hereby give the absolute right and permission to copyright and/ or publish pictures of me, in which I may be included in whole or part or composite or distorted, in conjunction with my own or a fictitious name, for advertising, trade or any other purpose whatsoever. I hereby waive any right to inspect or approve the finished product or advertising copy that may be used in connection with my photographic image.*

This release favors the photographer without considering the rights of the model. The Advertising Photographers of America National distributes a copyrighted "Model Release and Consent Agreement" with similar language. A professional photographer and member of the APAN explains it this way: "Releases are written like that to protect the photographer's rights to the photograph. It's standard. Models don't get paid if they refuse to sign."

If models sign such a release, they relinquish nearly all rights to the photos; if models don't sign, they have no control of the photos. This means, *models are damned if they do and damned if they don't!*

There may be a more equitable solution to this business arrangement between photographer and free-lance model. It seems reasonable that a free-lance models' rights should be protected without jeopardizing a job opportunity. Maybe the photographer's Release should read more like the one on the following page.

PHOTO RELEASE

For value received, I hereby grant _____

(photographer's name) permission to photograph me this day

_____ (date). This agreement extends to the specific use/

s as stated below, with limitations and not for all   purposes,

including unauthorized publication in whole   or in part,

whether blurred or altered, in composite or distorted in charac-

ter or form, in conjunction with or without a fictitious name.

I retain the right to reinspect and/or approve all subse-

quent usage of these photos for the sake of advertising, art, trade

or commerce.

MODEL'S NAME:_____

Purpose and/or usage of photos:

_____

_____

_____

_____

DATE:_____

PHOTOGRAPHER:_____

ADDRESS:_____

PHONE:_____

WITNESS:_____

This Release guards against misuse or exploitation of the model's photographed or filmed image, while allowing the photographer to apply his trade. Simple, fair and reasonable.

If you do not understand the language of a release, take it to someone who will help explain it. **Do not rely on the individual offering the contract to explain the content fully and accurately. Ask for copies of everything you sign.**
Would you sign a release which included the following statement?

In addition, as an added bonus, I agree to be put in the exclusive dating section of your magazine. Please check if unavailable _____. *[Confusing isn't it? Should your check the box, or not?]*

The photographer who offered such a cleverly worded release was later arrested and found guilty on five counts of pandering for the purposes of prostitution. Hundreds of young women had signed that release and left the "availability" box unchecked. When some of the young women were asked if they realized what they had signed, all said they did not.

✔ *RED FLAG ALERT:* **Lawyers will help you interpret contracts, or represent you in a wrongful action suit, but do not expect them to work for free. Minimum retaining fees can cost hundreds of dollars.**

CHECKLIST

✔ Does the release agree to let you (or your representative) authorize all blurrings, distortions or alterations?

✔ Does the release outline specifically for what purpose or possible purposes your photos will be used?

✔ Did the photographer provide you with a copy of the release?

✔ Did you *read it before you signed it* ?

6

PSYCHOLOGICAL PROFILES

PERPETRATORS, VICTIMS AND PARENTS

"If you bail me out, I promise to give you $8,000 worth of portfolio materials free!"—Jailed "photographer" to a model he tried to scam.

"I can't tell you all my secrets."—Glam scam "agent's" reply when asked how he went about getting work for models.

PERPETRATORS

Entertainment industry cons prey on basic psychological, emotional and economic desires of their victims. They dangle carrots of fame and fortune and lure their victims using advertisements or smooth talk to find the most vulnerable or needy individuals.

What personal characteristics make up a typical glam scam artist? Can you recognize one when you meet one?

Federal and local law enforcement sources offer these following tips on recognizing glam scam operators:

1. Glam scam operators are inflexible. They usually lose their cool and become abrupt and unprofessional if what they want doesn't happen their way.

2. Glam scam operators typically exaggerate. They offer ridiculous amounts of money and/or present fanciful schemes.

3. Glam scam operators often present exciting travel opportunities. Sometimes they offer to act as a personal escort.

4. They are evasive. Glam scam operators cannot answer a straightforward question.

5. Sometimes glam scam operators have an unprofessional appearance and/or lack of industry knowledge.

6. Glam scam operators are fly-by-night or like to save money by operating out of small, makeshift offices with sparse furnishings.

7. Most glam scam operators trigger an uncomfortable gut reaction from the very beginning.

8. Individuals who have nothing to hide invite you to check their references. A glam scam operator will typically be evasive if asked about their background.

9. Glam scam operators typically use props (cameras, scripts, celebrity photos, plaques, etc.), to give the impression of professionalism.

10. Glam scam operator's most often used defense is ignorance of the law.

✔ *RED FLAG ALERT:* **What glam scammers want to do to you they have already done to someone else.**

VICTIMS

Psychologists agree that desperation, vulnerability and intense competition are what create potential victims of glam scam victims.

> *"Many individuals who aspire to make it in the*
> *entertainment world feel a sense of consuming urgency*

*and desperation about their career as a performer. They
are convinced that this is the only endeavor that will
affirm their self-worth. This consuming need tends to
cloud one's judgement about the realistic circumstances
that one encounters throughout the search for success.
One tends to believe what one wants to believe, hence it
is helpful to document, as much as possible, your
interviews and auditions. Write down dates, names,
places and promises. Do your homework and check
thoroughly the reputations and credibility of the people
you deal with."*—**Edna Herrmann, Ph.D**, Clinical
Psychologist and Co-Chair of the Media Committee
for the Los Angeles County Psychological
Association

*"Potential victims are self-involved, immature,
lacking self-esteem, outwardly naive, needy to an
extreme and lack a direction in life. If this describes you,
counseling may be a helpful option."* —**Elaine Rodino,
Ph.D.**, Clinical Psychologist and past President of
the Los Angeles County Psychological Association
and current member of the Board of Directors.

*"Victims sometimes may be in denial and may
ignore basic red flag warnings. Talent and models need
to pay close attention to how people talk, since language
is a very revealing characteristic of people's values. The
entertainment industry attracts an overwhelming share
of sociopathic and psychopathic personalities, so talent
needs to be cautious. Sex is no guarantee of landing a
job."*—**Linda Durre, Ph.D.**, Psychotherapist

PARENTS
Parents need to be especially clearheaded and cautious.
Glam scams aimed at parents or children are almost always financial in nature. Perpetrators manifest opportunities which
exploit the desire of the child and the drive of the parent. This
doubly-vulnerable condition is ideal for the glam scam artist.

The three most common unethical glam scams targeted for parents/children are: national photo directories that promise too much, cost too much and are scarcely used by anyone in the industry; unsanctioned pageants that charge by the category and guarantee everyone wins; photographers who solicit work based on hospital birth lists or school district enrollment records.

STAGE PARENTS

*The following analysis of "stage parents" is contributed by media psychiatrist **Carole Lieberman**. Dr. Lieberman is Diplomate, American Board of Psychiatry and Neurology, Assistant Clinical Professor of Psychiatry at U.C.L.A., a member of AFTRA and the Writer's Guild*

Today, the temptation to make your child a 'star' is greater than ever. It can seem like the magical solution to your economic woes. And, it can hold out the promise of those 15 minutes of fame Andy Warhol predicted. But, if you become a 'stage parent' you could impair your child's psychological development and destroy your family's happiness.

You know you're a stage parent if you...

✔ Embark upon trying to make your child a star without finding out what your child wants.

✔ Insist upon trying to make your child a star despite your child having no interest in being a star or despite your child stating that he/she does not want to be in show biz.

✔ Always wanted to be a star yourself and are disappointed that you never made it, but hopeful that your child will.

✔ Believe that you can live vicariously through your child and enjoy the applause your child receives as if it were your own.

✔ Give your child's show business career priority over all his/her other needs—including: school, friends, hobbies, time for reflection, etc.

✔ Give your child's show business career priority over your needs and the needs of other family members.

✔ Bore or brag to other parents—and anyone else who will listen—about your child's talents.

✔ Harbor an unrealistic high appraisal of your child's talents, despite being told otherwise by several more objective professionals.

✔ Are willing to engage in unreasonably expensive and/or unethical practices to give your child's career a boost.

✔ Cling to the hope that if your child becomes a star it will solve all your problems and give meaning to your life.

Unscrupulous agents, managers, photographs and would-be producers know just how to prey upon "stage parents". They recognize that if you are a "stage parent", you are rather desperately pursuing stardom for yourself and just using your child as a means to that end. You may not be conscious of this, but unconsciously, at least, you are trying to do for your child what you wish your parents had done for you: made you a star. Unfortunately, your child will not appreciate your efforts as your child will know that they are not being loved unconditionally for who they are, but rather for the last chance at stardom they can potentially bring to you.

Instead, you can encourage your child to participate in drama, singing, dancing and musical instrument lessons. You can take your child to movies, plays, recitals, operas, ballets, etc. and bring your child backstage to meet the performers. But the desire to perform must emanate from the child. Unless your child has a sound foundation for good self-esteem—which comes from feeling unconditionally loved—your child will be psychologically scarred by the innumerable rejections which line the elusive path to stardom. Is the chance at stardom worth the risk of psychological damage? Whose chance at stardom is it anyway?... and whose psychological damage?

CHILD LABOR LAWS

Know the Child Labor Laws in your state. Call your state Labor Commission (or equivalent office) for information on employment of minors in the entertainment industry. Also ask for a list of available union/nonunion Studio Teachers.

The **American Federation of Television and Radio Artists** and the Screen Actors Guild offer a booklet called "The AFTRA-SAG Young Performers Handbook." This is a very accurate guidebook and a valuable resource for your entertainment industry library. Subjects covered include parental do's and don'ts, marketing tools, Child Labor Law summaries for the U.S. and Canada, on-set school requirements, a Glossary of terms and much more!

The **Hollywood Screen Parents Association** (HSPA) is a personal support and resource network for parents of child actors. Founder **Barbara Schiffman** publishes the *"Hollywood Screen Parents News,"* an informative and valuable newsletter. Other HSPA member benefits include a calendar of events, consultations, resource information, Speakers Bureau, Screen Parents Forum and industry-related directories.

> *"Parents should trust their own instincts and be especially cautious before spending hundreds or thousands of dollars on 'getting started' in show business,"* advises Schiffman. *She uses the example of modeling schools that have "auditions" from which students are selected for "partial scholarships." Schiffman points out that a series of expensive modeling courses will not help your child get work in movies or television, nor ensure modeling jobs.*
>
> *"Also, advertisements from personal managers seeking 'fresh faces' which run in local newspapers or parenting publications are generally not worth pursuing. There are so many kids eager to be in show business and so many low-cost or no-cost ways to find reputable agents and managers. The ones looking for "fresh faces" need your child—and your money—more than you need them."*—**Barbara Schiffman**, Founder, Hollywood Screen Parents Assn.

CHECKLIST

Perpetrators
✔ Do they seem unprofessional?
✔ Do they offer worldwide travel and/or big money contracts?
✔ Can they look you in the eye as they answer your questions?
✔ Do they offer references?

Victims
✔ Do you *need* to be in movies?
✔ Are you focussed on what you really want out of life?
✔ Do they want you to trade sex for a job?

Parents
✔ Have you asked your child what he or she wants?
✔ Have you made show biz the priority in your child's life?
✔ Is that cereal commercial your child was once in all you can talk about?
✔ Have you created an entertainment industry library?

7

WHO'S WHO

"If a person practices a licensed profession without a license, the law may clobber such a person."—Walter E. Hurst, "Manager's, Entertainer's and Agent's Book"

The business of entertainment is more specialized today than ever before. There was a time when booking agents and vaudeville theater owners controlled actor's and entertainer's performances and wages. Today, the business ethics, standards and practices of individuals who work with or employ talent are monitored by unions, guilds, professional associations/organizations and nonprofit consumer advocate groups. Since there are numerous entertainment related job titles, it is vital to know who's who and what they can legitimately do for you.

A costly mistake made by many people who want to be in show business is to have no idea of who's *who* —who can help, who could hurt. Likewise, many glam scam artists don't bother to do their homework. I once asked a "personal manager" from Hollywood, who was conducting a free seminar in Las Vegas, "Do you know the laws in Nevada regarding personal management?" His answer was, "No, but my lawyer tells me I'm doing nothing wrong here today." With that admission and unnecessary invocation of his lawyer, I knew he was selling something. The correct answer to my question was simply this: *There aren't any!* If I were an actor attending that seminar, I would have gotten up and left at that point.

✔ *RED FLAG ALERT*: **Know the law for your own protection.**

Following is a list of entertainment industry job titles that deal directly with talent. Each job description is followed by its licensing requirements and related union or professional industry affiliation.

ACTING COACH

Acting coaches are available in most areas. An acting coach is hired in several ways: by talent, by a producer or maybe by a director. The financial commitment to acting classes, offered by coaches, should be within one's means. The classes should be gratifying and developmental. No promises should be made by the coach or director of the acting class. There should be no "Hollywood hype" involved, says veteran Los Angeles and New York acting coach **Gerald Gordon**. If you hear, *"The only way for you to meet casting directors is to take my class,"* or; *"I know of a part that's perfect for you, but you'll have to take my class "* —go elsewhere! Gordon stresses to check credentials of coaches and teachers. "As far as your career goes, no legitimate acting coach can guarantee anything, nor will they!"

Fees and charges are unrestricted. Evaluate the value of the class by examining the reputation of the coach, subjects to be covered and time involved. Knowledgeable sources say classes should offer the opportunity to be acting in class almost all of the time. A good class should offer color videotaping sessions. Ask to sit in on the class. Ask the coach for free promotional materials. Many have handouts or preparation sheets with information on the class structure and coach's background. Give the class a fair chance. If after a few weeks you are not satisfied with your progress, try a new class.

Kevin McDermott's company, Center Stage L.A., conducts theatrical workshop classes for young performers. McDermott says, "It's very easy and inexpensive to make a few calls. Check anyone you may study with through appropriate unions/guilds and licensed agents. Trust your instincts—and trust your child's instincts! Be careful of out-of-towners. Never pay large amounts of money to someone who claims they can make you a star in Hollywood."

✔ *RED FLAG ALERT:* **Be leery of acting coaches or teachers who regularly introduce scenes of seduction or "sexual awakening".**

Beware of coaches or teachers who promote "secret" methods. Beware of long-term residential programs. Find out if the coach or teacher is presently a member of a performer's union. Where did they teach last?

Make sure the class is properly licensed by the state, county and/or city. Beware of schools that guarantee work upon completion. And beware of *"Anyone can be in commercials!"* sales pitches.

Licensing: a state nonprofit or profit license may be required; county or city license may be required if operating as a business.

Associations: None applicable.

BUSINESS MANAGER

A Business Manager is an individual, firm or corporation whose services include giving financial advice, and/or usually includes the management of talent's finances. Areas such as, managing investments, expenses, trusts, loans, wills, corporations, property acquisitions, divorces, lawsuits, insurance, taxes and criminal charges are usually handled by a Business Manager. Business Managers are most typically attorneys or accountants.

Business Managers are employed by talent and should be familiar with the business and financial aspects of the entertainment industry. For their services, Business Managers usually require around 5% of talent's gross earnings. Business Managers are often granted talent's power-of-attorney.

Richard deBlois, of deBlois, Mejia & Company, an accounting corporation based in Beverly Hills, California, says to ask your attorney for several Business Manager recommendations. When choosing a Business Manager, deBlois says to start by asking a few vital questions:

1. Is business management just a small part of their practice, or is it their speciality?

2. Will they handle all areas of your business management personally, or will some work be "farmed out"?

3. Do they have professional liability insurance?

4. Is their fee arrangement fair to you?

✔ *RED FLAG ALERT*: **Be very careful. You are entrusting business managers with your financial future!**

Licensing: Predominantly, licensed attorneys or certified public accountants (CPA). CPA/Business Mangers are usually licensed by the state. Business Managers who are not also CPAs do not require a state license.

Associations: None applicable.

CASTING COMPANIES

Legitimate casting companies are employed by production companies to provide talent for parts in films, television, commercials, music videos, etc. Casting companies work with talent agencies to offer producers choices of talent. Legitimate casting companies are paid by the production company—not by talent agencies and **never** by talent. Unlike talent agencies, casting companies usually do not require state employment agency licensure. A casting company is employed by a client (producer) to find suitable talent, which the client then hires directly or indirectly through a licensed talent agency.

In some cities, such as Los Angeles, Chicago and Vancouver, casting companies sometimes charge legal onetime registration fees to talent; some take a 10% commission; others charge a fee and take a commission. Casting is an unregulated service business.

These types of casting ads should send up immediate red flags:

✔   "Call 976-CAST! Just $2.50/call."

✔   "Hollywood Directors May Want You For Movies, TV, Videos...Send $10 for processing and handling."

✔   "Casting Call. No experience required...1-900-BE A-STAR!"

✔   "Extras & Stand-Ins...$60/month guarantees you work."

Casting companies are not regulated by a performer's union. The Screen Actor's Guild does allow casting companies to charge SAG members an annual $5-$15 photo fee. **DO NOT pay a casting company for a SAG membership card!** Membership into the performer's unions is earned through experience, not bought for a price.

There once was a union specifically for "extras," but the Screen Extras Guild was absorbed by the Screen Actors Guild in July, 1992. *Casting Services* are offshoot casting companies that find extras, atmosphere players, seat-fillers, audience members or background people! *Casting Services* sometimes find people by posting conspicuous flyers on telephone poles or newspaper racks:

ALL TYPES NEEDED IMMEDIATELY FOR EXTRA AND STAND-IN ASSIGNMENTS, MAJOR FILMS, NATIONAL COMMERCIALS, ROCK VIDEOS AND MODELING ASSIGNMENTS ★ —SAG WELCOME—	8833 Sunset Blvd. Suite 308 Los Angeles, CA 90069 310/555-8457 INQUIRIES ACCEPTED: M—F, NOON TO 6 P.M. ONLY.

Guarantees of work from *Casting Services* may involve becoming a paid audience member for an infomercial program. Infomercial audiences are paid around $50 to fill seats and applaud on cue. *Casting Services* usually require registration and/ or monthly fees. Do not confuse *Casting Services* with Casting Directors or casting companies. *Casting Services* are not employment agencies. *Casting Services* require a county or city business license.

What complicates matters is, anyone can set up shop as a *Casting Service*! **Dolores Chevron/FPA Agency** says, "'Casting Services is a fairly new term that says nothing and most likely is not legitimate. The people operating these services will show you letters and glowing reports from actors and directors that convince you that they are in a position to accelerate your career...they request rather large sums of money for the privilege."

The Network, a Hollywood-based, nonprofit actor's information and protection group with over 400 members, says they have discovered fee-charging *Casting Services* doing business out of residential garages and "crack houses".

Some *Casting Services* are complete frauds. They have no intention of ever casting a project, but collect fees anyway. Then, they close, move to another part of town under a different name and defraud people all over again.

Sometimes in Hollywood, when a *Casting Service* goes out of business, they sell all headshots on file to thrift stores and souvenir shops. Store owners then put the photos on display in boxes for tourists and fans to purchase. The thought is, that photograph may be worth something when yesterday's unknown becomes today's hot movie or TV star! After all, Tom Selleck, Suzanne Somers, Kevin Costner, John Travolta, Bruce Willis, Dustin Hoffman, Jack Nicholson, Julia Roberts and many other stars were once "extras."

✔ *RED FLAG ALERT*: **Beware of casting companies or services that charge commissions and/or take money for registration, classification, categorization, filing or postal fees.**

Licensing: no state license or bond required; county or city business license usually required if operating as a business.

Associations: (See Casting Director)

CASTING DIRECTOR

Essentially, a casting director screens and presents talent choices for various roles. A casting director is employed by a casting company or as an independent contractor for a film, television or other producing company. Talent should never pay a casting director any money.

Anyone can call themselves a "casting director." Ask for credits and then verify their background and references.

Casting directors assemble types: blue-collar; girl-next-door; high-fashion; villain, etc. They also offer extras. Casting Directors do not manage talent and should not offer talent to exclusive representation agreements. **Legitimate casting directors do not charge talent registration fees!**

One of the most common abuses is the unauthorized use of the "Star Search" name or logo. Not just anyone can get you on "Star Search."

The guy with the video camera who says he's a "Star Search" casting director, is the equivalent of the guy with a disposable camera who says he's a *Playboy* photographer!

"Star Search" employs only a few casting directors, whose job it is to attend closed auditions across the country. According to the show's producer, "Star Search" does not authorize use of the show's name or logo for contests and does not get involved with contests that charge fees. Here is an audition ad for "Star Search" contestants. Notice the specific mention of their host (Ed McMahon) and their talent search sponsor (Snapple).

★   **Star Search**   ★
Talent Hunt

Ed McMahon's Star Search starts its eleventh successful season this fall and we're looking for the next generation of talented entertainers. We will be kicking off "Snapple Presents: Ed McMahon's Great American Talent Hunt" here in Los Angeles on July 30th.
Want to audition?
★   Call 1-800-662-0880   ★

Beware of casting directors who will not tell you the company they work for or the product being represented.

✔ *RED FLAG ALERT:* **Beware of casting directors, no matter who they work for, who ask you to work for free. They may be in violation of Federal minimum wage laws.**

Licensing: no individual license or bond required; no state, county or city license required.

Association: Casting Society of America (C.S.A.) The C.S.A. is an industry union with nearly 300 members.

PERSONAL MANAGER

Personal Managers are employed by talent. A Personal Manager guides and coordinates the business and career activities of talent. A Personal Manager advises and counsels on long-term career choices, matters of public image (including dress, makeup, interview techniques, etc.), develops projects for talent and sometimes runs the talent's personal production company. Personal Managers also assist talent in the selection of other support professionals, such as agents, attorneys, business managers and publicists. A primary responsibility of a Personal Manager is to stay in constant contact with the talent's agent.

A 1985 report from the California Entertainment Commission, which was comprised of three performers (Edward Asner, John Forsythe, Cicely Tyson), three Agents (Jeffrey Berg, Roger Davis, Richard Rosenberg) and three Personal Managers (Bob Finklestein, Patricia McQueeney, Larry Thompson), concluded that the essence of a Personal Manager's service "is counseling the artist in the development of his/her professional career."

State of California statutes read that Personal Manager commissions are totally negotiable. In 1983 the California Legislature concluded that "Although their functions frequently intersect, personal managers and talent agents are distinguishable professions." The 1985 California Entertainment Commission report stated: "No person, including personal managers, should be allowed to procure employment for an artist in any manner or under any circumstances without being licensed as a talent agent." The Commission also concluded that "there is no need for a separate licensing law for personal managers."

Personal Managers should take no more than 15% of talent's gross pay. A good rule of thumb, according to author and career counselor Linda Buzzell, is that a Personal Manager (or agent) should be able to raise your income by at least the percentage that you are paying them.

Personal Managers should not promise talent work, charge monthly fees, actively seek employment opportunities for talent or imply the guarantee of jobs. Read personal management contracts very carefully.

Personal Manager and former Conference of Personal Managers Secretary, Michael Harrah, advises: "If a personal manager asks for money up front—run the other way!"

National Conference of Personal Managers President, Gerard W. Purcell, specifically warns that "anytime a personal manager asks for any money up front for anything— including photos, vocal or acting classes, video resumes, etc.—consider that individual unscrupulous."

The **Los Angeles Office of the Consumer Protection Agency of the Federal Trade Commission** warns that "personal management companies do not usually advertise for newcomers and never promise employment."

Do not confuse *"Talent Manager"* (or "Talent Representation company") with Personal Manager. (See Talent Manager)

Licensing: no individual license or bond required; no state license required; city or county license required if operating as a management company.

Associations: The Conference of Personal Managers, Inc. (COPM) is a professional organization based in Los Angeles with approximately 70 members. The COPM guarantees its members are professional and offers a hotline with suggestions and recommendations on hiring a Personal Manager. The hotline number is a recording which asks you to leave your name and number and also asks you to give them permission to call you back collect.

The National Conference of Personal Managers (NCPM) has 230 members with offices in New York and Los Angeles. The NCPM promotes and protects the rights of both Personal Managers and their clients (talent) with a code of business ethics and standards which members must abide by. Check out Personal Managers with the NCPM by sending your inquiry and a stamped, self-addressed envelope.

✔   *RED FLAG ALERT*: **A personal manager should have provable industry connections and complete knowledge of the marketplace, including employment laws, union agreements, licensed agencies, etc.**

PHOTOGRAPHER

Photographers get referrals from many sources: talent agents; personal managers; casting directors; unions; professional associations; and word-of-mouth. Referrals from agents, casting directors, producers and/or consultants, should include choices. If a certain photographer's name is recommended by various sources, consider that photographer credible.

Association of Talent Agents (ATA) Executive Director, Chester L. Migden, advises to "Check out *all* photographers! Ask for references."

Know the cost of the session. Know what is included in the session (number of shots, number of free prints, wardrobe changes, who owns the negatives). Ask when the proofs will be ready? How much are "test prints"? When will you receive the prints?

You are paying for the session, so tell the photographer what you want out of the pictures. Be specific and assertive. (Even if you are not paying for the session, know what type of photo you will and will not take.) When working with photographers, maintain a professional attitude.

Guidelines for Working with Professional Photographers

✔ Headshot sessions should take 1-2 hours.

✔ Headshot sessions can range from $50-$150, which usually includes 3-6 outfit changes and a dozen or more poses. Proof sheets are included, but negatives are usually not included. Fees for a professional makeup artist are also not usually included.

✔ A "proof sheet" or "contact sheet" allows talent (and agent) to choose which photograph or "look" is best to use as a headshot.

✔ A photographer should provide proofs in a week or less.

✔ Order a test print to see how the headshot will actually look. This is sometimes an added expense, but well worth it.

✔ The photographer should offer dry matte originals, glossies and/or lithograph copies. Additional custom prints bought from the photographer can range from $2-$12 per picture; glossies (used most often for theatrical submissions) can cost $45-$65 per 100 copies; litho copies (used mainly for commercial submissions) range from $45-$75 per 500 copies. Both printing processes normally take a week. Originals are mostly used in professional portfolios and as backups. Litho copies are acceptable most anywhere in the country. Laser print copies are also accepted by most agencies, supplemental to litho copies.

✔ Since it is the photographer's work being duplicated, it is in his or her best interest to know which photo duplicating services offer the best quality. Normal turnaround time for photo duplications is about a week.

Keep in mind that photographs are open to subjective judgment. There may be occurrences where what an agent likes, a casting director may not and both may disagree with your choice of headshot. These occurrences do happen. The only guarantee you will get with any type of photograph is this: *you cannot satisfy everyone.*

Beware of agents or personal managers who recommend only one photographer. When a photographer is being forced on you, it is almost always because the photographer is giving the agent or manager a kickback. Never use a photographer just to please an agent.

Do not let a photographer talk you into unnecessary semi-nude or nude shots that he claims, "no one will ever see." If you are uncomfortable with the photographer, for any reason, leave!

Beware of agencies or casting companies that say you can choose your own photographer, but the photographer must provide a written guarantee that the agency will approve of the photos. This is unreasonable and not standard practice.

A photographer may ask you to sign a "Model Release" form. READ IT CAREFULLY BEFORE YOU SIGN IT! *(See Releases section)*

A warning from the **American Guild of Variety Artists**: "Don't be fooled by flashy publications that will publish your headshot and promise you the moon."

Be leery of photographers who tell you, *"I don't work through agents because they just rip you off!"* Do not trust agents or photographers who tell you that their "headsheets" (a poster of faces, which you pay to be on) are the best way for you to be seen by people in high places. Headsheets are not the most effective marketing tool for talent. Talent agencies and photography studios sometimes produce headsheets simply as a way to supplement their own income.

Do not trust photographers who offer their models wine "to help relax" in front of the camera. Be wary of photographers who solicit you for "portfolio work". You may hear, "How about if I take some shots for your portfolio...Usually I charge, but I'll make an exception for you!" If a photographer claims to free-lance for all the major magazines ask that photographer to name exactly which publications he works for. Then, make calls to local agents, professional photography associations and the magazine publishers.

The most potentially harmful line you may hear from someone pretending to be a photographer is, *"Don't tell your parents, they'll only try to talk you out of it."* The most overused come-on line by unscrupulous photographers is: *"I CAN GET YOUR PICTURES TO PLAYBOY."*

Neil K. Spotts, Manager of Western Region Security for *Playboy*, says it is "very frequent" that a scamming photographer uses the *Playboy* name. *Playboy* Investigators handle many cases where young women call *Playboy* "after the models have gone through a lot of emotional hell, or sometimes have even been physically attacked," says Spotts. His advice is to check out all photographers who represent themselves as free-lance *Playboy* photographers. There is nothing wrong with calling any regional *Playboy* office. In fact, *Playboy* expects it.

The best way to be seen by *Playboy* is to be seen by *Playboy*! Any young woman of legal age can call *Playboy* and make an appointment—at no cost. Call the Los Angeles or Chicago *Playboy* offices on Monday for an appointment the following Thursday. The first six callers at each office receive an appointment with an honest-to-goodness *Playboy* photographer at the *Playboy* studios. For further *Playboy* submission policies, complaints or verification of a photographer, contact the Playboy regional offices: Chicago: 800-621-4105; Los Angeles: 800-238-5104; New York: 212-688-3030.

✔   *RED FLAG ALERT*: **Photographers cannot guarantee that agents or producers will like your photographs.**

Licensing: no individual license or bond required for photographers; no state license required; city or county license required if operating as a business.

Associations: none applicable.

PRODUCER

All the essential elements of the production, from the idea to distribution, are assembled by the producer. The producer is involved in obtaining the script, signing the stars and director and hiring all other personnel. The producer's job also involves selecting locations, arranging schedules and overseeing the budget. A producer employs talent. Producers approve casting and sometimes exercise their power by casting roles themselves. Sometimes a producer abuses this privilege. Do not trust producers who "cast" at cocktail parties. This is sometimes referred to as "Cocktail Casting".

Beware of sound-a-like companies. These are operations that use names similar to well-known studios or production companies to make you believe they are affiliated.

From the Hollywood Reporter (6/28/91): "*Scam uses Swayze name to defraud wannabe actors.*" Hundreds of young, aspiring actors across the country were promised movie roles by "Patrick Swayze Productions". All the actors had to do was send $300 to the company for "union dues." Over a period of nine months, this scam swept through Chicago, Boise, Milwaukee, Phoenix, Toledo, Cincinnati, Louisville, Memphis, Sacramento, San Diego and under the name "Rob Lowe Productions" in other cities.

None of the performers unions sell memberships through the mail. **Never send or give money to anyone who promises you membership in a performers union, without checking with the union first.**

On the following page is a flyer from another glam scam production company that set up shop for an assault on the unsuspecting.

☆ **APPEAR** ☆
IN A
MOVIE!
NO EXPERIENCE NECESSARY
NOW CASTING

People of every imaginable
age, size, shape and description.
People just like you!

THIS COULD BE THE START TO AN
EXCITING CAREER IN THE FILM BUSINESS!

FAMILY, COMEDY—ADVENTURE
FEATURE FILM
Auditioning is easy
Call 24 Hours-A-Day
☆ **1-800-767-7944** ☆
Tahoe Star Entertainment

This was the mailer and promotional handout of Tahoe Star Entertainment. This company invited "people of every imaginable age, size, shape and description" to be in the movies!

Look inside their slick brochure and there are catchy headings emblazoned in red ink:

> APPEAR IN A MOVIE!
> NO EXPERIENCE NECESSARY!
> THE MOVIE BUSINESS IS FUN!
> THE EXPERIENCE OF A LIFETIME!
> *and . . .*
> *participation fee*

What was that again? *"PARTICIPATION FEE"* ? The company brochure explained it this way: *"A wide variety of activities, such as dance classes or youth and adult sports leagues require the payment of a participation fee. In much the same manner, we charge a **nominal participation fee** for appearing in this production. The par-*

ticipation fee is very reasonable, only $75. This fee is used to help offset the cost of producing the film." In legitimate production circles a person who shares in the financing of a project (and profits) is called an Executive Producer. It is doubtful that is what this company had in mind.

There's more. According to Tahoe Star Entertainment's contract, sending the company $75 did not guarantee you would appear in their movie. Your "investment" also did not guarantee proper credit if you were chosen to appear in a scene by their producer and/or director. In one paragraph, Tahoe Star Entertainment's Appearance Agreement and Release says: "Talent will receive end credit for appearance." The very next paragraph says, "should end credit be omitted or talent's face not appear . . .no refund of participation fee will be given."

A few phone calls revealed that Tahoe Star Entertainment was based in Colorado Springs, Colorado, but incorporated in Reno, Nevada. The company was operating with a post office box, an 800 number (with a lengthy recording) and a cellular phone. Talk about mobile! Fortunately, before summer's end, Nevada enforcement officials had forced Tahoe Star Entertainment out of business.

> *Ed. Note: A recent article on casting in a leading videography magazine offered low-budget producers the worst possible advice. The article suggested that video producers hang flyers wherever people congregate or stand in line, such as markets, gas stations, public restrooms or movie theaters! The article also strongly suggested the use of classified ads to find talent. A thousand times NO!*

Charles B. FitzSimons, President of the Producers Guild of America, advises to "ask straightforward questions of persons representing themselves as producers. Legitimate companies have nothing to hide. Check a producer's credits with the Producers Guild, or other reliable sources."

Beware of independent producers who want to sign talent to multi-picture deals—but the talent only gets paid when ALL the films are completed.

Beware of out-of-state production companies that advertise for talent or models. "Never give money *for any purpose* to a producer," says **Chester L. Migden, Executive Director of the Association of Talent Agents**.

✔ *RED FLAG ALERT* : **Anyone can call themselves a "producer." But one question can legitimize or betray a producer: *"What have you produced?"***

Producers Beware! You can also be a target of money scams. Be careful of whom you deal with. Financing schemes involving highly-skilled money launderers are rampant the entertainment industry. Studios, experienced producers and tyro producers are susceptible to "financier" glam scams.

If it is their money they are investing, the deal should be relatively simple: They give you the cash, you make the movie. They control someone else's money, or represent a trust, overseas investment company, anonymous investor, etc., be extra cautious. It is this second scenario—someone else's money—that the "deal" may involve expense advances, matching funds, elaborate arbitrage transactions, margin acquisitions, certificates of deposit, bonds, letters of credit, escrows and other cmplex and somtimes purposefully confusing transactional elements.

✔ *RED FLAG ALERT:* **If the deal involves "other people's money," enlist the assistance of an experienced attorney, accountant and trusted banker.**

Licensing: no individual license or bond required; usually, a state, county or city license and bond is required for any company operating as a motion picture producing company. (A reminder: just because a production company is incorporated, licensed and bonded, it does not necessarily mean they are legitimate.)

Producers Guild of America (PGA): 400 members. The national union for producers of motion picture and television productions.

STUDIO TEACHER

Studio Teacher-Welfare Workers are exclusive to California. Studio Teacher-Welfare Workers hold valid and current California Elementary and Secondary teaching credentials and are certified by the Labor Commission. Besides teaching on the set, Studio Teachers are responsible for the health, safety and morals of all-age children during production. A Studio Teacher Availability List can be obtained from the Alliance of Motion Picture & Television Producers (AMPTP), or Los Angeles Local #884.

"Tutors" are not the same as Studio Teacher-Welfare Workers. Sometimes "Tutors" are simply relatives or friends asked to baby-sit.

Polly Businger, Los Angeles Local No. 884 Business Agent offers three simple ways to verify Studio Teachers:
1. Studio Teachers give report cards;
2. Studio Teachers sign the back of the child's entertainment work permit;
3. Studio Teachers are listed with the Labor Commission or Los Angeles Local No. 884.

Licensing: Valid and current state of California Elementary and Secondary teaching credential and Labor Commission certification.

Associations: Los Angeles Local No. 884.

TALENT AGENT

Agents represent many types of talent: actors and actresses, models, singers, dancers, toddlers, kids, teens, ingenues, specialty acts, animals and animal acts, performance artists, narrators, writers, directors, producers, cinematographers, sports stars, and other professional performers.

According to the California Talent Agencies Act, "talent agent" is the accepted statutory term for an entertainment industry employment agency. The *Hollywood Reporter* calls the California Talent Agency Act "the model for similar statutes in numerous other states" (*Hollywood Reporter* , "Hollywood Guilds Fend Off Talent Agency Deregulation Plan, 9/2/92). The Talent Agency Act, as stated in California Labor Code, Section 1700.4, defines a talent agency as *"a person or corporation who engages in the occupation of procuring, offering, promising or attempting to procure employment or engagements for* [talent]." Section 1700.5 stipulates that *"No person shall engage in or carry on the occupation of a talent agency without first procuring a license therefor from the Labor Commission."* California's Talent Agency Act has been in effect, in various forms, since 1913.

Here is a brief history of California's talent agency laws:

1913—The Employment Agencies Act included the servicing of a new industry with "theatrical employment agency" regulations, which covered circus and vaudeville acts, theatrical entertainers, exhibitors and other performers.

1937—The establishment of another employment agency category: "The motion picture employment agency."

1943—"Artists Manager" was added as a regulated category.

1959—The categories of employment agent, theatrical employment agent, motion picture employment agent and artist's manager are shuffled from government agency to government agency.

1978— The Talent Agencies Act was drafted and remains in effect today. "Talent Agent" becomes the accepted statutory term for an entertainment industry employment agency.

1982— Creation of the California Entertainment Commission by the California legislature; designed to recommend to the Governor and legislature changes in the Talent Agency Act, regarding the   licensing of agents. The Commission consisted of 10 members appointed by the Governor.

1985— a summary from the California Department of Industrial Relations determines that anyone, including personal managers, seeking to procure employment for [talent], needs a license.

1992—The Governor considers a proposal to repeal the licensing of talent agents. The plan receives no support from the entertainment industry and is scrapped.

1993— Legislators want criminal penalties put back in the Talent Agency Act. In 1982, the California Entertainment Commission had determined that criminal penalties were an ineffective method of dealing with unlicensed agencies. The resolution receives little support from the entertainment industry.

Talent agents offer talent contracts on behalf of producers. Talent agents also negotiate contracts and working conditions on behalf of talent. Fourteen states now have similar laws specifically addressing the licensure of *theatrical, talent, booking, modeling* or *entertainment* agencies. Other states, districts and Canadian provinces require a county or city business license. Talent and modeling agents operate with competitive commission fee structures. The current general industry standard is fifteen percent. *(See State-by-State section)*

Some talent agencies are "franchised" by performer's unions. This means the agency agrees to abide by all employment provisions and contracts as stipulated by performer's unions.

Union contracts stipulate that a **Screen Actors Guild (SAG)** franchised talent agent can take no more than a 10% commission from talent's wages.

In order to qualify as a franchised talent agency, the agency must fulfill all state, county or city licensing requirements and agree to abide by all union rules and regulations. According to the "Screen Actors Guild Codified Agency Regulations," Rule 16(g), Section VIII: Disciplinary Provisions, some of the violations which may subject agents to disciplinary action are: willfully violating SAG regulations; employing a non-franchised person as a sub-agent; sharing commissions; fraud or dishonest conduct; charging more than a 10% commission for talent's services; the "acceptance of 'kickbacks' or referral fees on photography, printing or any other services from any source providing such services." SAG's Agency Regulations also state: *"Agents shall not advertise through newspapers, magazines or mailings to the general public seeking clients for representation, registration or other forms of representation involving the payment of any fees directly or indirectly in the form of commissions, registration fees, referral fees or otherwise."* For complete agency requirements, agreements and basic contracts, obtain the "Screen Actors Guild Codified Agency Regulations".

The **Screen Actors Guild** advises the following: "Make sure your agent is franchised before signing an agency contract or accepting verbal representation; never sign contracts that contain blank spaces or missing information; improper behavior by a franchised agent should be reported to the SAG immediately (all reports are confidential). SAG does not have jurisdiction over print work or modeling and does not regulate personal managers. DO NOT PAY ANYONE FOR A SAG MEMBERSHIP CARD!"

The nonprofit professional organization **Women In Film** recommends reading the *Screen Actors Guild Codified Agency Regulations*.

✔ *RED FLAG ALERT:* **Be familiar with the contracts, rules and regulations of performer's unions and guilds.**

> "Check with your local licensing board regarding the legitimacy of agents. If there are agents franchised by the Screen Actors Guild or AFTRA in your area, they should be your first choices. Do not give money for anything—pictures, classes, etc.—to an agent, manager or whomever for a promise of representation."
>
> "In the field of modeling remember there are height and age requirements with legitimate agencies. Do not get a portfolio before getting an agent. In the larger cities the legitimate agents will see new talent for modeling (not acting) with a selection of snapshots. If you call a model agent and they do not give you height

and age requirements, be wary!

If you are signed by a model agent, they will recommend 'test' photographers for your portfolio. The agent should not recommend one photographer and you do not pay the agency, you deal directly with the photographer. 'Test' photographers charge a lower rate since they are looking to build their own fashion portfolio. The photographer owns the negatives, you do not. They will give you prints for your portfolio after you and the agent have selected the ones you want.

Don't answer ads looking for models and always try to find out about the reputation of the agent you are going to see."—**Nina Blanchard**, The Nina Blanchard Agency

✔ *RED FLAG ALERT* : **Ask the agency (or agent) how they plan to best use your talents. If they are consistently vague, consider another agency.**

"Beware of agents demanding a fee before you can work. Never pay a fee in advance to any agent or manager. Beware of licensed or unlicensed agents and photographers working together to get talent to buy unnecessary photos or portfolios. Do not send money to anyone who promises membership in any of the performer's unions. There are no short cuts to the top."—The **American Guild of Variety Artists (AGVA)**

"A legitimate talent agency does not charge a fee payable in advance for registration, resumes, screen tests, photographs, acting lessons or any other services. Legitimate talent agencies normally do not advertise for clients in newspaper classified columns nor do they solicit through the mail. If a so-called talent agent sends you to a particular photographer for pictures, hold your wallet tight and run for the nearest exit! Chances are the "agent" is a phony who makes money splitting the photographer's fee."—**The Los Angeles Office of the**

Consumer Protection Agency of the Federal Trade Commission

Beware of photo pushers. These are seemingly legitimate talent agencies who make money by receiving kickbacks from photographers. The agent's advice may sound helpful, but the photo "deal" will cost an exorbitant amount of money. For instance, an agent may say: "Only deal with photographers who will give you your negatives." Good advice. The agent may also say: "Beware of agencies that refer only one photographer." Excellent advice. The agent then offers you a choice of four photographers; three have competitive session prices, but do not offer you the negatives. The one photographer who does include the negatives in the price of the headshot session charges $450! Guess who gets a cut.

Be aware of the lawful maximum commission a talent or modeling agent can take in your state (see State-by-State). Some agencies may purposefully represent themselves as *personal management companies* and charge a greater commission than what is lawful.

✔ *RED FLAG ALERT:* **Legitimate agents get paid a commission only after talent is paid for a job.**

Licensing: some states require licensure of talent agencies; county or city license required if operating as a business. (See State-by-State section)

Association of Talent Agents (ATA): 120 members. A professional organization based in Los Angeles.

TALENT CONSULTANT
Talent Consultants are service based companies. Ideally, a worthwhile Talent Consultant should combine the industry knowledge, contacts and intentions of an agent, personal manager and casting director. For a one-time-only reasonable fee, Talent Consultants should offer advice on photographs and photographers, cover letters, resumes, mailings and interview techniques. They should know the path to take to make it in the

industry. A Talent Consultant is a facilitator, at best. Their service should answer many questions and ideally save novice actors and performers time and money. A Talent Consultant should never make promises or guarantees.

Talent Consultants should offer economical (and legal) shortcuts. They should have knowledge of discount services. A good Talent Consultant will supply current lists of franchised agencies and advertising firms where *you* can send or deliver your own pictures and resumes. Reputable Talent Consultants should not offer to submit your photos for you. **Do not pay a Talent Consultant to deliver your photos and resumes to agencies!** Beware of Talent Consultants who strongly suggest monthly advising sessions for a fee.

Licensing: no state license required; county or city license required if operating as a business.

Associations: none applicable.

TALENT COORDINATOR

A talent coordinator organizes talent for a production. Talent coordinators are employees of producers or production companies. If they do not represent a company, they cannot help you.

✔ *RED FLAG ALERT:* **If a talent coordinator approaches you, do not give out any personal information. Give him/her the name of your agent, or call the show's producer.**

Licensing: none.

Associations: none applicable.

TALENT MANAGER

What is a Talent Manager? Only a Talent Manager seems to know for sure! One thing is clear: "Talent Managers" and "Talent Representation companies" specialize in offering free come-one-come-all seminars...

```
General
        MODELLING—TV
      COMMERCIAL—FILM
Top Hollywood manager seeks new
clients to represent in LA market.
Kids, teens, adults. Free seminar:
Breaking into Hollywood.Personal
evaluation, Friday,Aug. 6th 7:30 PM
Cambridge Suites 1601 E. Flamingo
Rd.Reservations call 818/555-3001
```

Notice the "General" listing? This Talent Manager wants to reach as many people as possible, so he/she can "personally evaluate" who would be most likely to pay for expensive photo or resume services!

Licensing: county or city business license usually required. An employment agency license may be required in some states.

Associations: none applicable.

TALENT SCOUT

This job title has become relatively obsolete in today's industry. Producers, directors, agents, personal managers and casting directors are always on the look out for new talent— they are sometimes even paid a "finder's fee"—but very few people make their living exclusively as a finder of talent.

Anyone can call themselves a "talent scout". Here's a company looking to hire a "talent scout":

```
        ★ ★ Talent Scout ★ ★
No time clock. unlimited income. 80+ offices
across the country. Looking to open 3 in
Vegas area. We need fast learners to train
into management. Serious inquiries only.
        ★ ★ 255-3605 ★ ★
```

This company is not even in the entertainment industry. They sell health and beauty care products and were "scouting" the area for talented sales people.

RED FLAG ALERT: **The next time someone introduces themselves as a "Hollywood Talent Scout", ask them, "And what is it you do for a living?"**

Licensing: none.

Associations: none applicable.

Keep in mind, pictures of celebrities on a wall does not necessarily mean that photographer, agent, manager, producer, consultant, coach—*or whomever* —knows that celebrity!

HOW IT WORKS

The entertainment industry operates with many unwritten rules. Job responsibilities overlap and laws are vague. Learn the business side of the entertainment industry. One of your best and most reliable resources is other talent. *Call* other talent or models for their recommendations of agents, managers, attorneys, producers, pageants, contests, classes or other industry advice. Good word-of-mouth is essential to the reputation and credibility of any individual or company in the entertainment business. If word circulates that the *So-and-So Agency* pushes photos, or that the *Ms. Mr. Miss Pageant* reneged on contest prizes—those operations will not be operational for long.

The chart on the following page shows how it works (parentheses indicate talent's financial commitment):

HOW IT WORKS

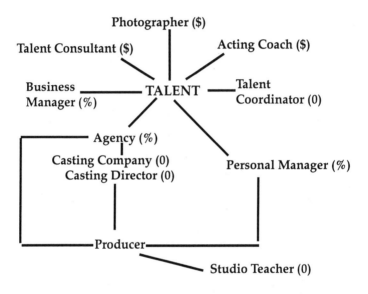

Legend: $ = service for a fee
          % = service for a commission
          0 = no financial involvement

CHECKLIST

Acting Coaches
- ✔ Does the class offer color videotaping?
- ✔ Will the coach or teacher allow you to audit the class?
- ✔ Does the coach or teacher offer mysterious methods?
- ✔ Are you satisfied that the coach or teacher is qualified?
- ✔ Do the local talent agencies recommend the class?

Business Manager
- ✔ Is the Business Manager familiar with the entertainment industry?
- ✔ Did you speak to your attorney before granting the Business Manager power-of-attorney?
- ✔ Are you prepared to entrust this Business Manager with your financial future?

Casting Companies
- ✔ Are they a *Casting Service* ?
- ✔ Do they charge a registration fee? (Is this legal in your city, county and/or state? See State-by-State section)
- ✔ Does their office look like a permanent business?
- ✔ Are they operating through the mail?
- ✔ Do they guarantee work?
- ✔ Are they selling union membership cards?
- ✔ Are the local licensed talent agencies familiar with the casting company?

Casting Directors
- ✔ Is he/she charging a registration fee?
- ✔ Do they have verifiable credits?
- ✔ Do they choose not to reveal information about the project for some mysterious reason?
- ✔ Do they want you to work for free?

Personal Managers
- ✔ Is there a compelling reason why they should want more than 15% of your gross wage?
- ✔ Do they promise work?

✔ Do they ask for money in advance?
✔ Did you find them through an advertisement in the local newspaper?
✔ Do they represent at least one recognizable client and have they adequately proved their knowledge of the entertainment industry, including employment laws and union regulations?

Photographers
✔ Did they invite their "employees" or friends to watch your photo shoot?
✔ Did you meet them while shopping at the local mall?
✔ Is their equipment professional?
✔ Does the wardrobe for the shoot match the product?
✔ Do they insist that you need a composite card?
✔ Do they claim they can get your pictures to *Playboy* ?

Producers
✔ Do they want you to pay to be in their movie?
✔ Do they become defensive when you ask for their credits?
✔ Do they have production money in place and a start date, or are they just casting *for the hell of it* ?
✔ Do they want to be starmakers instead of movie producers?

Studio Teachers
✔ Is the Teacher licensed and certified by the state?
✔ Was the Teacher referred by a state referral office or local union list?
✔ Is the Teacher looking out for the health and welfare of your child?

Talent Agencies
✔ Do they want money for services in advance?
✔ Did the agent tell you (or your child) that you *need* to be on television?
✔ Do they guarantee employment?
✔ Do they recommend only one photographer?

✔   Are they primarily picture pushers?

Talent Consultant
✔   Do they want you to come back and keep paying them for consultation fees?
✔   Have they been down the path they are sending you?
✔   Is their agency list current?
✔   Do they insist it is best that they submit your picture and resumes?

Talent Coordinator
✔   Do they actually work for a production company?
✔   Did they ask for personal information?
✔   Are they reluctant to tell you the name of the show's producer?

Talent Manager
✔   Do they hold free seminars to the general public and offer personal evaluations?
✔   Are they required to be licensed to do business in your state, county and/or city?
✔   Do they imply representation?

Talent Scout
✔   What is it they really do for a living?

8

TIP-OFF TO RIP-OFF

"I can't refer calls to the Labor Commissioner..."—California Department of Labor representative

How can you identify a glam scam? Who should you call first? It depends on the circumstances. Familiarize yourself with the functions of each of your recourse options, before you call to register a complaint. Keep a journal. Notate dates, contact names and numbers, requests and responses. That way, if licensing and/or enforcement officials need to become involved, they can work from your notes instead of your memory.

✔ *RED FLAG ALERT*: **Licensing does not necessarily mean legitimacy.**

Protect yourself. Be pro-active , not reactive! The key is to investigate the individual or company before you make a decision, not after it is too late.

Here is an alphabetical summary of some of the offices you could call. Keep in mind that state, county and city government and special enforcement offices are closed on weekends.

ATTORNEY GENERAL

Call the state Attorney General's office when you have been the victim of a fraud or suspect an unscrupulous business dealing. The Attorney General takes action against individuals or companies harmful to people of the state.

The Attorney General refers complaints to other related agencies—Consumer Affairs, film commission, area Better Business Bureau, etc. The Attorney General's office usually will not release complaints made against a company, because that may jeopardize an ongoing official investigation of that company.

BETTER BUSINESS BUREAU

Call the Better Business Bureau to inquire about the business reliability and practices of a member business. Call to register complaints or to inquire if any complaints have been made against a member company. The Better Business Bureau will offer rules of thumb, case studies and past histories of similar business operations. Better Business Bureaus are public, nonprofit, non-government agencies with no enforcement nor prosecuting powers. The Better Business Bureau has reports available warning about hundreds of scams and how to avoid them. For instance, the **Council of Better Business Bureaus** distributes "Tips For Consumers" information to all Better Business Bureau offices. "Child Modeling Scams: Parents Beware", in particular, warns to avoid companies that require up-front fees for registration, consultation or administration services.

The **Los Angeles Better Business Bureau** fields approximately 20 calls a week related to talent agents, casting offices and other entertainment companies. They refer nonmember inquiries to the state Labor Department.

The Los Angeles Better Business Bureau advises talent to get all promises in writing. They stress that legitimate talent agencies do not guarantee work. Also ask for references, read all contracts carefully, and investigate the company.

CHAMBER OF COMMERCE

Call the Chamber of Commerce to check a business' standing in the community. Chambers deal with established businesses. Since most unscrupulous business operations are fly-by-night, Chambers of Commerce are not usually involved. By no means should the Chamber be the only call you make.

The **Hollywood Chamber of Commerce** has a 45-member board that reviews new member applications. The Hollywood Chamber may withdraw member status for inappropriate business conduct. Conduct does not have to be illegal, only unprofessional, for member cancellation.

COMMERCE DEPARTMENT

Call the State Commerce Department to check on an individual or company that offers an overseas job opportunity. They may direct you to a consulate, embassy, international trade office, or even the FBI.

CONSUMER AFFAIRS

Call Consumer Affairs (Public Protection Agency, Bureau of Investigation) or equivalent office, when you have been misrepresented by a service, product or claim from an individual or company. Consumer Affairs gathers information, but does not enforce. Usually, Consumer Affairs prepares complaints for action by the state Attorney General or city District Attorney.

Consumer Affairs can only prepare complaints for action which apply to their jurisdiction. Complaints outside their authority are a very low priority. Your state, county and/or city may have a Consumer Affairs office. While some Consumer Affairs offices can share information upon inquiry, others are lawfully prohibited. This means, there may be complaints, *but they can't tell you!*

Laws and how they are written can sometimes thwart the efforts of a Consumer Affairs office. In California, for example, modeling agencies are thought to be licensed by the state Labor Department, when in fact, they are not. California Labor Code, Section 1700.1(a):

"Theatrical engagement" means any engagement or employment of a person as an actor, performer, or entertainer in a circus, vaudeville, theatrical, or other entertainment, exhibition, or performance."

Nowhere does the California Labor Code include or define "modeling."

Enforcement is a separate problem. What good is a law if state, county or city authorities are unable to enforce that law? Los Angeles County Consumer Affairs has seven investigators to assist over nine million people in Los Angeles County!

Just one more reason why talent and models need to protect themselves. No one is going to do it for you.

✔ *RED FLAG ALERT:* **Do not rely strictly on the reports of government agencies or consumer affairs offices.**

CONSUMER REPORTER
Call a newspaper or television consumer reporter to offer information on a fraudulent individual or business. Reporting on rip-offs is part of their service to the community, besides being good for ratings.

Still, many other news items—fire, car crashes, political scandals, drive-by shootings, etc.—can take precedence over an entertainment-related rip-off.

COUNTY/CITY BUSINESS LICENSES OFFICE
Call the appropriate business licensing office to verify the license of a business. Ask how the business is specifically licensed. Business licensing regulations and enforcement procedures vary from county to county and city to city. Some counties and cities do not regulate commercial businesses. Generally, anyone offering a product or service for sale or trade must possess a form of business license. Also, call the licensing office to register complaints.

FILM COMMISSION
Call the state, county, or city film office for industry related information and updates. Call for current licensed agency lists and / or to register a complaint.

LABOR DEPARTMENT
Call the Department of Labor (Labor Commission, Labor Board, Labor Regulation Division) or equivalent office for

employment laws and regulations in your state. Call if you have a complaint against an employer. Municipal regulatory offices rely on rulings and actions of state Department of Labor offices.

Most Department of Labor offices are understaffed. These offices are notoriously slow in reacting because of the volume of complaints.

NATIONAL FRAUD INFORMATION CENTER

Call the National Fraud Hotline, 1-800-876-7060, Monday—Friday, 10 AM—4 PM EST for general advice, enforcement referrals and/or when you need assistance in filing a formal complaint. The Hotline provides fraud updates and tips on how to avoid scams. You can also talk to a staff member. This private nonprofit organization does not regulate, but will forward your complaint to the proper authorities for investigation.

The National Fraud Information Center cannot advise on specific businesses or individuals.

POLICE

Call the police when you believe a crime has been committed, or is in the process of being committed. Be sure to have all the facts, including names, addresses and circumstances. The police need facts not conjecture.

Contact the divisions of Vice, Bunko, Fraud or Missing Persons. Police divisions share information from state-to-state and work closely with the FBI. The police may be unable to share complaints about a specific company or individual because that may jeopardize an official ongoing investigation. Keep in mind, special departments are closed on weekends.

PROFESSIONAL ASSOCIATION

Call a local professional association or nonprofit industry watchdog group to double-check the reputation of an individual or business. Often, associations require membership to use their services. Small membership dues can be worth the support. Nonprofit organizations are usually fair and objective and not intimidated by illegal operators.

Perhaps there is a nonprofit professional organization in your area.

SECRETARY OF STATE

Call the Secretary of State to check on a corporated or incorporated business. Call to register a consumer complaint. They may refer you to another related agency.

Generally, the Secretary of State's office cannot offer any more information than the principle officers listed on the application, the company's address and whether the company's incorporation fees are in good standing.

STUDIO OR PRODUCTION COMPANY

Call a studio or production company to verify a production, employee or someone's claimed affiliation with the company. If someone tells you they are with a certain television show, call the show's producer and check it out. It may only take one phone call.

UNION/GUILD

Call a professional union or guild office regarding rules and regulations, contracts, franchised agents, pay schedules, complaints and other talent related inquiries. Most unions and guilds require membership to utilize their services.

CHECKLIST

✔ Author's advice: Be preventative so you do not have to rely on others to take recourse on your behalf.

9

SCENARIOS

Wanted: Live-in. Female models only. Millionaire will pay all expenses. Travel and penthouse. Once in a lifetime opportunity —actual classified ad seen in a free entertainment newspaper

Six typical glam scam case studies are presented here. They are all based on true cases. Test your awareness. How many warning signs can you find?

CASE STUDY No. 1: Desperate and vulnerable...

You have just been laid off at the bank. You have applied elsewhere, but have no solid offers. The rent is due. The car payment is overdue. A collection agency needs a minimum credit card payment. You need money.

You remember this guy, a banking customer. He asked if you had ever modeled and said you had the "look". He works with models every day, but he had never seen anyone like you. He handed you his business card. You remember he said his models make $150 a day. He guaranteed that you could make that too, probably more! You search for his card.

You find it. It looks like this:

CLASS MODELS
& TALENT ENT.

Worldwide photographers
800-555-CLAS

"Slim", Modeling Manager

At first glance it looks pretty good. Now you remember this guy. His teeth matched his wrinkled, brown, ill-fitting suit. Oh well, one-hundred and fifty dollars is one-hundred and fifty dollars, right?

Maybe you should ask someone, see what they know about Class Models & Talent Enterprises. Or does the "Ent." stand for Entertainment? You call the Better Business Bureau, who can report no complaints against this company. You call 800-555-CLAS and get a recording. It says to call 1-900-555-2000 to find out how Class Models & Talent can make you $150 a day as an elite model. The call will cost you three dollars for the first minute. You justify it as an investment.

The recording goes something like this:

Welcome to the elite world of modeling. You have been discovered by one of our trained modeling managers. This automatically qualifies you to make a guaranteed $150 a day—or more!—As one of our elite group of exclusive high fashion models. Not everyone has what it takes to be a model, but we know you do.

We work with photographers worldwide. Some of our models have graced the pages of magazines you may avidly read . . ."

After another minute of happy-talk, you finally get their photographer's name and number in your area. You call the photographer and make an appointment for later that day. He gives his studio address and tells you to bring jeans, formal wear, a swimsuit and "something sexy."

Not ten minutes go by when you get a phone call. It's the photographer. He suggests meeting him instead at a park for some location shots. "Come to think of it," he says, "maybe you'd feel more at ease, since you're new at this, if we did the photos at your place." You agree.

He shows up forty-five minutes late. And he smells bad, as if he ran over as fast as he could. He's holding an off-brand 35mm camera. You invite him inside and nervously explain your reason for doing this. He grins benignly and explains the $20 categorization fee. You give him cash. He says when he sells your photos you'll get a check in the mail.

He takes his first shot with the lens cap still on the camera. He laughs it off, says "say 'cheese'" and snaps a couple of headshots. Before you know it, you've changed into your swimsuit. He takes some pictures of you posing in the living room. "How about some sexy ones?" he suggests. Though you know you shouldn't (you have a nagging gut feeling he's a sleazeball), you allow him to take a few "tasteful" pictures of you nude.

He finishes the roll of film and digs in his pockets for more. "Darn," he says, "I left all the other film at my office. I'll be right back." You never see him again.

The next day, you try calling his office, but no one ever answers. You call Class Models & Talent Ent., but can't get a live voice. You're very angry because you feel exploited. You call the police.

Analysis of Case Study No. 1:

How many "red flags" or misjudgments did you spot? There are 23. Let's start with your disposition. You're vulnerable, desperately in need of quick and easy money. You think back to a business card you were handed at the bank. You can't remember the guy's name, but recall his compliment. He guarantees you can make big money...

The name of the business is incomplete ("Ent."). His business is described as "Worldwide photographers", whatever that means. He has a singular, funny nickname, creative job title and an 800# number. You also remember his unprofessional appearance. You check out the company with the Better Business Bureau, which is a stab in the dark. The 800# turns into a 900#. You waste money listening to a recording. The word "elite" is over-used, as if Class Models & Talent Ent. is attempting to align it-self with the renown Elite Model agency. The recording does not say exactly which magazines Class Models & Talent Ent. ever worked with, then wastes more of your time with fluff.

The photography representative suggests a meeting at a location outside his studio. He even takes it a step further by recommending a one-on-one session at your residence. He ar-rives late, smells of body odor and doesn't even offer a business card. He has a substandard 35mm camera, no lights, no special setups and later we find out, only one role of film. You give him cash up front (you could have at least written a check). You sign no Release form and agree to the verbal terms. He seems incom-petent (e.g. lens cap). You are uncomfortable during the entire shoot, pegging him for a creep. He leaves with what he came for: your money and some nude photos to sell.

Has there been a crime committed? No. You agreed to the condition that *"when "* your photos are sold, you will get paid. That could be next week or fifty years from now, accord-ing to the verbal agreement. There was no sexual abuse. You are of legal consenting age and invited him into your residence. You agreed to the topless photos. Yes, you were exploited, but you have little legal recourse.

CASE STUDY No. 2: Don't tell your parents...

You see an ad in the Saturday classifieds which reads: *"MODELS—hot, young girls 16-20 wanted for exciting, new nat'l tanning product. Lic. #004. No selling req. Call Terry, 555-2009, ext.432."*

It's the middle of the afternoon. It's summer, your par-ents are away and you're bored.

You have always been interested in modeling. Four years ago, you were Miss Little Teen. You call the number.

A woman answers, "Dive Motel..." You ask for exten-sion 432. After about ten rings, a man answers. He sounds groggy, as if you woke him up. You tell him you're calling about the ad in the paper for models.

"How old are you?" he asks.

"Seventeen."

Suddenly he's awake and charming.

"What's your name?"

You tell him. He says it's his favorite name in the whole world. He then tells you about the product. He tells you how he has traveled around the world for the product, looking for the right girls. He is the international casting coordinator for the product, which is based on the East coast.

"Do you know who Cindy Crawford is?" he asks.

"Of course," you reply.

"I got her her first job. Do you know Christian Slater?

"Sure."

"He's my cousin...Anyway, come over, let me do some test shots and we'll see what we get."

"I have to wait until my parents get home."

"Why? Do you need a ride? I could —"

"I have a car, it's just that —"

"They'll only talk you out of becoming famous."

"Well, okay."

You go to the interview.

Analysis of Case Study No. 2:

This scenario might take about ten minutes to unfold. How many red flags and errors in judgement are there? Fifteen. Is there a crime here? Chances are, there will be.

She's bored and thinks modeling is easy. She answers a weekend classified advertisement for underage females. If she would have waited until Monday, she could have found out that "Lic. 004" was meaningless. Extension 432 is obviously a motel room. Even though it is midday, he was sleeping. The first question he asks is her age. He smooth talks her, dangles the carrot of travel. He has an impressive sounding job title. He name-drops. Again, she could have waited and called her local SAG branch and asked about this "cousin." The photographer was very eager to pick her up. He tells her not to tell her parents. She goes to the interview alone.

CASE STUDY No. 3: The talent search . . .

Universal-Foxx Productions is holding a "Star Search for Talent" contest, Saturday and Sunday only, at a local nightclub.

There is a $25 entry fee. You get a talent analysis, a free 8 X 10 and could qualify for over $4,500 worth of photographic and video contracts, make-overs and other portfolio materials.

Analysis of Case Study No. 3:
Sounds great! There are six "red flags" in this come-on. This company sounds like a combination of two well-known motion picture/television studios. They are using the "Star Search" name in the title of the contest. Are they licensed to do business and accept fees in your county or city? What is a "talent analysis"? Who is judging the contest? What are the particulars on the contracts, make-over and portfolio materials?

Is this legal? Maybe, maybe not. If they have been granted a business license, they can operate. Buyer beware.

CASE STUDY No. 4: Free talent evaluation...
You notice an ad under "General" in your local newspaper's classified section. It reads:

> **Actors, Models**
> Hollywood talent management co. conducting free seminar, Saturday 8pm. Looking to represent new talent. Free evaluation. No exp. nec. Worldwide exposure. Call 800-555-6565.

You make a reservation.

Saturday evening comes and you attend the seminar. A woman who calls herself "your Talent Representative" flashes several 8 X 10 photos of actors and models she "discovered." She claims their actors and models are making tens-of-thousands of dollars a day! "You can too!" she says. She tells her audience of over 100 people a few more personal Hollywood discovery stories. She then gives some general how-to advice and concludes with a video about her company. You then step in line for your free talent evaluation.

When you sit across from her, she asks if you brought any pictures. You show her a professionally done 4X6 and 8X10 black and white headshot. She glances at it; asks where you had it done. You tell her a local photographer. "Not good," she comments and adds, "This won't work in L.A. or New York City, or even Chicago." She says you have a fresh, marketable look, but your photo is worthless. It needs to be redone.

Her photographer will be back next week, you should make an appointment, says *your Talent Representative* . Her photographer will make you a "commodity in the larger, more commercial markets." You ask how much it will cost. "I could get you calls immediately, with better photos—that's how quick it can happen. Believe me, you could do very well!" But how much does the photo session cost, you ask again.

"Six-hundred and fifty dollars." It's a short-term investment in a long-term career, she explains. "Do you know how much commercials pay?" she says too excitedly.

You pay for the photo session and wait a week for the promised proofs. Two weeks go by, so you call *your Talent Representative* . . . You call everyday for another week, but get only a recording telling you she's out of town. You call the photographer, but his phone is no longer in service. Now what do you do?

Analysis of Case Study No. 4:

Eleven "red flags". The classified ad was placed under "General," indicating that this company wanted to reach as many people as possible. The name of the company was not included in the ad. The interview takes place on a weekend and in the evening (when city, county and state licensing and special enforcement offices are closed). If they "represent" talent for employment in or out of your state, they may require specific licensing in your state and/or county or city. "No experience necessary" is a classic come-one come-all pitch. They are operating using an 800 number exclusively.

Your Talent Representative, an erroneous title, offers some free and sensible advice, but your personal evaluation hits a snag: a non-workable photo. She suggests her photographer. With her photographer, a lucrative career in commercials is all but guaranteed! How much will it cost? Your Talent Representative shows reluctance in answering a direct question. So, you pay up-front for very expensive headshots that you will never get, because *your Talent Representative* and photographer are suddenly unreachable.

You'll need more money (long distance phone calls, attorney, travel, etc.) and a lot of time to get the photos or your money back!

CASE STUDY No. 5: In need of investors...

An independent producer needs a few million more dollars to launch his maiden film project. Sources of money are unavailable; the well is dry. So close, yet still so far. Miraculously, he gets a phone call. One of his "feelers" has come through! A motion pictures *financier,* also known as an investment facilitator or liaison, has a possible "matching funds" deal. The *financier* has access to a pool of money from various investment sources—including "offshore" money. He has between $12-20 million to move. But specific conditions must be met: 1) The investment group wants only bankable stars and directors involved in their projects; 2) They request a synopsis of the film, completed script, producer's bio, letter of intent from the "stars" and a 5% financing fee payable in advance before any money is put into escrow.

"What's your budget?" asks the *financier.* The producer says he only needs around two million dollars more. "I'll run it by the Board," says the *financier.* The producer offers more details on the project.

Twenty-four hours later, the producer gets a call from the *financier.* The *financier* says the Board loved the project and not only approved the financing, but they waived the usual 5% finance fee. The producer can have access to four million dollars within 7-10 days. All the *financier* needs is $4,500 "good faith" money; cash, no check. The *financier* arranges a meeting "to get the ball rolling."

The next morning, they meet in a pancake house. The *financier* is officious, casually dressed and carries a briefcase and cellular phone. He begins the meeting with, "So, do you have the cash?"

Analysis of Case Study No. 5:

Did the "financier" need to hold a sign that said "SHY-STER"? These types of scenarios always produce countless "red flags". Sometimes, a producer's sensibilities are blinded by a desperate desire to get the project made—at any cost! "Investment facilitators" exist everywhere. They talk the talk, *then walk with your money!*

CASE STUDY No. 6: The VIP...

The town is excited about the big, blockbuster movie coming to film, Fox Film Corporation's remake of "Rebel Without A Cause," starring Tom Cruise. The Location Manager will arrive in the next few days. When he does arrive, he asks for a complimentary room, and gets it. He asks for a complimentary rental car, and gets it. He also places a classified ad in the local newspaper—open auditions for the female lead! Interviews will be conducted by appointment only, in his hotel room.

Analysis of Case Study No. 6:

There are six obvious "red flags" in this familiar scenario. "Fox Film Corporation" is a sound-a-like company that most likely has nothing to do with "Rebel Without A Cause" (a Warner Bros. copyright) or Tom Cruise. A call to the Warner's studios and Tom Cruise's agent is required. The "Location Manager" asks for everything free. This is unprofessional. Lastly, and most importantly, why is a Location Manager conducting a casting call for the *female lead*, in his hotel room?

He's a fake, a fraud and odds are harmful.

10

STATE-BY-STATE

"If you wait for it to become a problem, it will."—Wendol Jarvis, Iowa Film Commissioner

In 1984, serial rapist and murderer Christopher Wilder crossed the country kidnapping, raping, torturing and killing numerous innocent women, before being captured by police in Colebrook, New Hampshire. Wilder usually approached young women in malls, representing himself as a fashion photographer.

There are currently 175 U.S. and 47 international film commissions located throughout the world. A 1992 survey of film commissions across the U.S. and Canada revealed that a vast majority of states, counties, cities and provinces have had serious problems with entertainment industry scam artists, in the last ten years. That's a lot of glam scam activity! **Leigh von der Esch**, President of the **Association of Film Commissioners, International** (AFCI), urges: "If you feel unsure about an offer or opportunity, pass on it."

Three factors significantly contribute to the likelihood of glam scam operations in your area: regulatory laws, enforcement, and local newspaper policies.

Regulatory laws for talent and modeling agencies differ from state to state. Only a handful of states have specific "entertainment agency" (i.e., talent, model, theatrical or booking) licensing requirements. Most states operate with more general "private employment agency" regulations, while a few states have no laws which apply to the employment of talent and/or models. Though states may not regulate the employment of talent, individual counties and cities usually have their own regulations in the form of codes and/or business licensing requirements.

Hollywood, **California**, the "Motion Picture Capital of the World," has no business licensing requirements. That's because Hollywood is not an incorporated city, it is a district within Los Angeles County.

In Clark County, **Nevada**, wherein lies the city of Las Vegas, "Sin City," where many think prostitution is legal (though it isn't), it is unlawful for licensed modeling agencies to advertise using any of the following or similar phrases:

The utmost in discretion
You won't be disappointed
We come to you
Dating service
Showgirls-models-actresses-hostesses
College girls, models, dancers, etc.
Group discounts
All our models have health certificates
Call anytime
24 hour instant service
Fox hunting
We deliver
You always win
We have a model for your every need
Models to act out your fantasies

Models in the privacy of your hotel or motel room
Warm
Friendly
Pleasant
Nude models
No hidden costs

The **Minnesota** Department of Labor has a recording answering most often asked questions. **Texas, Nevada, New York, Arkansas, Illinois** publish and distribute cautions to talent and models on how to avoid scams. To become licensed as an agent in **Arizona, Delaware, Pennsylvania** or **Washington** individuals must pass a written exam. Some states bar talent agencies from advertising for a position unless one exists. Depending on interpretation, this may lawfully prohibit "new faces" types of ads in those states. Some state laws are specific, while other state laws are vague.

But what good are rules if there is no enforcement? Sure you have recourse, but if no one takes swift and meaningful action against illegal operators what's the use? Each state reacts differently to complaints. Some states try to prevent the problem with community awareness efforts. A few states have undercover operations.

✔ *RED FLAG ALERT:* **What are the laws in your state?**

The map on the following page shows each state's regulatory laws as related to talent/modeling agencies.

The amount an agent can take from talent as a commission also varies from state-to-state. Thirty-seven states and the District of Columbia do not restrict talent agency commissions. Four states—Maryland (20%), New York (10%), Pennsylvania (10%) and Washington (20%)—lawfully limit talent agency commissions. Two states—California (15-25%) and Arizona (15-20%)—adhere to what their respective Labor Commissions call "Unwritten Standards". Seven other state's employment agency laws apply to maximum allowable talent agency commissions— Alaska (10%), Iowa (15%), Louisiana (15%), Mississippi (15% commercials; 10% feature films), Oklahoma (15%), Oregon (5%)

and Wisconsin (15%). The industry standard across the country averages fifteen percent.

Glam scam operators use local newspaper classified ads because it is the most effective way to reach the greatest number of people for the least amount of money. Do not assume newspapers operate with complete knowledge or understanding of city, county or state licensing laws. Do not assume an ad is legitimate just because it is printed in the newspaper.

Some newspapers offer disclaimers and/or cautions. Still, the liability for answering the ad is yours. Local newspaper editors and/or classified advertising managers can dramatically curtail glam scam activity in your area, if they would verify necessary licenses before publishing a classified ad! *(See Classified Ads section)*

Information on employment laws is available from the U.S. Department of Labor/Employment Standards Administration, Wage & Hour Division, 200 Constitution Avenue NW, Washington D.C., 20210, 202-523-7406. This is a helpful and accessible office.

Also, the *National Fraud Hotline* is a good place to start if you need directions on how to file a complaint. *(See Who's Who section)*

Following are summaries of talent agency laws from state-to-state. State laws can be open to interpretation. This section should be used as an overview, not as a definitive legal source. Any similarities of abridged classified ads to real ads does not imply nor necessarily suggest that the ads came from an unscrupulous source.

ALABAMA
Does Alabama have a problem with entertainment scams: Yes.

How problems are solved: The Film Commission handles complaints personally. They check out new agencies and utilize state, county, and city licensing divisions, and local police. If necessary, the film commission will involve the state Bureau of Investigation, and/or Attorney General.

Talent and Modeling Regulatory Laws
State-by-State

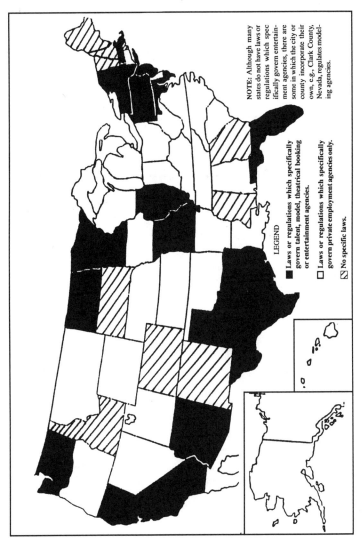

NOTE: Although many states do not have laws or regulations which specifically govern entertainment agencies, there are some in which the city or county incorporate their own, e.g., Clark County, Nevada, regulates modeling agencies.

LEGEND

■ Laws or regulations which specifically govern talent, model, theatrical booking or entertainment agencies.

□ Laws or regulations which specifically govern private employment agencies only.

▨ No specific laws.

Licensing: Alabama does not have specific laws which regulate talent/model agencies. Employment agencies must be licensed by the state Department of Revenue. Employment agency applicants must have been a resident for at least two years and have two years related experience. No bond is required.

Newspaper: The Birmingham News

Published Disclaimer: "The publisher reserves the right to classify ads under their proper heading, and to revise, reject, or cancel any advertisement at any time, when deemed necessary."

Sample Ad:

---

241 Modeling/Talent
HOLLYWOOD AGENCY to scout/
hold workshop 8/15 Univ. Inn.
All ages.

SAG office: None

Film Commission: Michael Boyer, Director, Alabama Film Office, 401 Adams Avenue, Montgomery, Alabama 36130; 205-242-4195; 800-633-5898; FAX 205-242-0486.

Attorney General: 205-242-7300

ALASKA
Does Alaska have problems with entertainment scams? No.

Licensing: Alaska does not have specific laws regulating talent/modeling agencies. Employment agencies must be licensed by the Department of Labor. Licenses can be denied if there is reason to believe that the applicant is "irresponsible." Agencies cannot operate out of residences. All advertisements must contain the agency name and address and identify the advertiser as an agency. Agencies can charge registration fees not exceeding $2; "Sale of job information" $1-$5; resumes $50-$200, and a lawful maximum 10% commission for temporary placement. An agency cannot charge both a registration fee and a resume fee. A bond is required in the amount of $10,000.

Newspaper: Anchorage Daily News

Published Disclaimer: None specific to employment agencies.

Sample Ads: None.

SAG office: None.

Film Commission: Mary Pignalberi, Director, Alaska Film Office, 3601 C Street, Suite 700, Anchorage, Alaska 99503; Tel 907-562-4163; FAX 907-563-3575.

Wage & Hour Administration Department of Labor: 907/269-4900.

ARIZONA
Does Arizona have problems with entertainment scams? Yes.

> *5/25/92: Jack McLean, the "Gentle Rapist," faces 30 years in prison for sexually exploiting two adolescent girls in Arizona. He is also suspected of sexually assaulting more than 60 young women throughout Florida during the '70s. In Phoenix, he allegedly billed himself as a photographer and distributed fliers soliciting models.*

How problems are solved: Attorney General.

Licensing: Arizona has laws which specifically apply to talent/modeling agencies. Talent and modeling agencies must be licensed as an employment agency. Employment agencies must be licensed by the Department of Labor. Agents must pass a written test. Agencies cannot charge registration fees (unless approved). The unwritten standard talent agency commission ranges from 15-20%. Agents cannot advertise except for bona fide positions. All advertising must contain the agency name. Agencies must provide detailed and specific employment contracts. Artist/Agent contracts cannot exceed two years. A bond is required in the amount of $5,000.

Newspaper: Arizona Republic

Published Disclaimer: none.

Sample Ads:

> "*Models all looks/ages: photo, modeling, tv, magazines, swimwear. Free promotion. Member World Modeling Assoc. Call Starmaker.*"

> "*Model and talent search. Los Angeles agency interviewing all ages for models, film, commercials, tv, experienced or not.*"

> "*Models/Dancers. 18yrs. & older. No experience nec. Call for info.*"

> "*Models, actors, entertainers: Major talent & model search by top talent scout for modeling, fashion, movies, commercials & magazines. Be reviewed by industry professionals in AZ, NY, CA, Europe, Japan. All ages, looks, sizes. Free promotion, details! Starmaker.*"

SAG office: 1616 East Indian School Road, Suite 330, Phoenix, Arizona 85016; 602-265-2712

Film Commission: Bill MacCallum, Director. Arizona Motion Picture Development Office. 3800 N. Central Avenue, Bldg. D, Phoenix, Arizona 85012; 602-280-1380; 800-523-6695; FAX 602-280-1384.

Industrial Commission/Department of Labor: 602/542-4515

ARKANSAS
Does Arkansas have a problem with entertainment scams? Rarely.

How problems are solved: Better Business Bureau and Attorney General. The state film office distributes printed cautions to talent and models.

Licensing: Arkansas does not have specific laws regulating talent/modeling agencies. Employment agencies must be licensed by the Department of Labor. To be eligible for a license, agents must possess the equivalent of a twelfth grade education in terms of "intellectual competency, judgement and achievement." All advertisements must state that it is an employment agency. Agents cannot use aliases. Agents cannot ask talent for power-of-attorney. Agencies cannot charge fees "for any service other than actual placement." A bond is required in the amount of $5,000.

Newspaper: The Arkansas Democrat-Gazette

Published disclaimer: None.

Sample ads: None found.

SAG office: None.

Film Commission: William Buck, Director. Arkansas Motion Picture Development Office, 1 State Capitol Mall, Room 2C-200, Little Rock, Arkansas 72201;501-682-7676; FAX 501-682-FILM.

Department of Labor: 501-682-4541

CALIFORNIA—Los Angeles
Does California have a problem with entertainment scams? The film commission does not involve itself in this area.

> *6/10/93: Wallace Kaye, a licensed and franchised Hollywood talent agent received a five year, four month jail sentence and $1,500 fine for sexual attacks on 11 actresses and models. The Judge ruled that the agent took advantage of the women's trust and followed a "premeditated scheme."*

How problems are solved: No response.

8/20/92: Governor Pete Wilson considers deregulating talent agents. State legislators say the state spends upwards of $200,000 annually to pursue legal disputes involving talent agencies.

4/29/93: The Talent Agency Act is under scrutiny again as state legislators seek to restore criminal penalties to the Act. If passed, operating an agency without a license would be a misdemeanor, punishable by fine and/or imprisonment. Criminal penalties were removed from the Act in 1982 when the California Entertainment Commission determined that such penalties did little to restrain illegal activity.

Licensing: California has specific laws regulating "talent agencies." Talent agencies must be licensed by the Department of Labor. All advertising must contain the agency name, address, the words, "talent agency" and license number. Agencies cannot collect a registration fee. The unwritten standard talent agency commission is 15-25%. Agent/Artist contracts can include a provision which allows the agent to "advise, counsel or direct the artist in the development or advancement" of talent's career. Fingerprints are required for licensing. Agencies must pay talent within 15 days of receiving payment from the client. A bond is required in the amount of $10,000.

Newspaper: The Los Angeles Times

Published Disclaimer: "The *Times* reserves the right to refuse to publish any advertisement, to correctly classify any advertisement and to delete objectionable words or phrases. For additional policies and standards of acceptability contact: Department of Advertising Acceptability, 213-629-4411, ext. 76131 or 76148."

Sample Ads:

"Models sizes 12-18. Spectacular Models. No fee/ guaranteed."

"Models—Kids/Adults for nat'l commercial. No fee. Employment not guaranteed."

"SAG film. Open call Sat-Mon. No photo fee, employment not guaranteed."

"Kids needed for adult roles. Free auditions for kids to play young versions of police/firemen/nurses, etc. All colors, ages 3-23. No experience necessary. If qualify, representation guaranteed. 100% placement (small fee). Employment not guaranteed. Actors Unlimited."

"Actors and Models Wanted. Int'l Talent Search. American/Euro/Asian/ Latin types, all ages. Immediate exposure TV, movies, commercials, print. Call for free screen test and interview now! Telecast systems. No photo fee. Employment not guaranteed."

SAG Office: (National Headquarters) 5757 Wilshire Blvd., Los Angeles, CA 90036-3600; 213/954-1600.

Film Commission: California Film Commission, Patti Stolkin Archuletta, Director, 6922 Hollywood Blvd., Suite 600, Hollywood, California 90028; 213-736-3456; 800-858-4PIX (US & Canada); FAX 213/736-2522

Los Angeles Film Commission: City Of Los Angeles Entertainment Industry Affais; Cody Bluff & Jonathan Roberts, Co-Directors, 6922 Hollywood Blvd., Suite 614, Hollywood, California 90028; 213-847-2948; 213-461-8614; FAX 213-847-2949

CALIFORNIA—San Francisco

Newspaper:
The San Francisco Chronicle/Examiner

Published Disclaimer: (see advertisementon following page)

Sample Ads::

"Models/Actors. Not a school. Print, commercial, ramp. Call now."

"Licensed acting and modeling. Private and semiprivate instructor available for tv commercials, drama, runway, high fashion photography. Promo and management. 7 days."

"You can be seen by the World's top agents with John Robert Powers, SF experts for 47 years. Train in fashion shows/magazine modeling and tv/film acting! No experience! All types/sizes. Free evaluation."

"Be discovered! Top New York agency "Next Models" scout comes to S.F. Powers Modeling School one day only to find new faces! All types, no experience. Call for free screening NOW!"

SAG Office: 235 Pine Street, 11th Floor, San Francisco, California 94104, Tel 415-391-7510

California Film Commission: (see main California commission under **California—Los Angeles** listing)

San Francisco Film Commission: Lorrae Rominger, San Francisco Film and Video Arts Commission, Mayor's Office, City Hall, Room 200, San Francisco, California 94102, 415-554-6244, FAX 415-554-6503

CALIFORNIA—San Diego
Newspaper: The San Diego Union-Tribune

Published Disclaimer: "All copy must be approved by the newspaper, which reserves the right to request changes, reject, or properly classify an ad. The publisher reserves the right to cancel any ad at any time."

Sample Ads:

> *Models—$125/hr. SD/LA agent now accepting new talent. All looks, all ages, all races. Movie extras, print, tv. No fee. License #2878."*

> *"Jobs in Japan. For singers, dancers, models, and special talents. Paid round-trip airfare, apartment, and visa arrangements. Now interviewing for departures."*

> *"Models—$750/day. New York fashion catalog house seeks men, women, and children for new collection. No fee."*
> *"Actors—Models, all ages needed. TV commercials, print. State Licensed Talent Agent."*

> *"Models/Actors needed for TV commercials. 10% commission."*

> *"Model auditions. Men, women, children. Fashion shows, photo, tv.*

Part-time, good pay, no experience. Creative Arts Modeling Agency. Lic. #0864."

"Swimwear Illustrated cover search. $$ + trips to Europe, Caribbean, Brazil."

"Start modeling today. Call . . ."

"Management company looking for fresh faces. We believe in quality not quantity, and personality counts."

SAG Office: 7827 Convoy Court, Suite 400, San Diego, CA 92111; Tel 619/278-7695

California Film Commission: (see main California commission under **California—Los Angeles** listing)

San Diego Film Commission: Wally Schlotter, Director, San Diego Film Commission, 405 West Broadway, Suite 1000, San Diego, California 92101; 619-234-3456; FAX 619-234-0571

Department of Labor: 415-703-4750

COLORADO
Does Colorado have a problem with entertainment scams? No.

Licensing: Colorado does not have specific laws which regulate employment agencies (which includes talent/modeling agencies). Certain regulations pertaining to employment agencies are imposed and enforced by the District Attorney (Consumer Affairs Section) from county to county.

Newspaper: The Denver Post

Published Disclaimer: "All ads are subject to the approval of this paper which reserves the right to edit, reject or properly classify any ad."

Sample Ad:s

SAG office: 950 South Cherry Street #502, Denver, 80222, 303-757-6226; 800-527-7517.

Film Commission: Michael Klein, Director. Colorado Motion Picture & Television Commission 1625 Broadway, Suite 1975, Denver, Colorado 80202, 303-572-5444; FAX 303-572-5099.

Small Business Assistance Center: 303-592-5920

CONNECTICUT
Does Connecticut have problems with entertainment scams? No.

Licensing: Connecticut does not have specific laws which regulate talent/modeling agencies. Employment agencies must be licensed by the Labor Commission. Agencies must provide talent with receipts of employment. Agencies cannot charge advance registration fees. All advertisements must include the determination of "Fee Paid" or "Applicant Paid," if such charges apply. A bond is required in the amount of $7,500.

Newspaper: Hartford Courant

Published Disclaimers: "The *Hartford Courant* attempts to screen all ads for validity. For your protection, please note that these positions should not require any payment from the applicant, and some positions may be considered independent agents and would require the applicant to file the appropriate tax information. Also, 900 phone numbers charge a fee if dialed." And: "The *Hartford Courant* reserves the right to refuse or reject any advertisement... In no event shall the *Hartford Courant* be liable for consequential damages of any kind."

Sample Ads: None.

SAG office: None.

Film Commission: Rena Calcaterra, Director. Connecticut Film Commission 865 Brook St., Rocky Hill, 06067-3405; Tel 203-258-4301; FAX 203-529-0535.

Attorney General: 203-566-2090

DELAWARE
Does Delaware have problems with entertainment scams: No.

icensing: Delaware does not have specific laws which regulate talent/modeling agencies. Employment agencies must be licensed by the Division of Business and Occupational Regulation. Employment agencies cannot advertise a position unless one exists. Agencies cannot charge advance registration fees. Agents must pass a written examination. A bond is required in the amount of $5,000.

Newspaper: The News Journal

Published Disclaimer: "All ads are subject to approval before publication. We reserve the right to edit, refuse, reject, or cancel any ad at any time."

Sample Ads:
"*Modeling—Acting. John Casablanca's Modeling Center and Vineland Studios of Hollywood seek new faces for modeling, TV commercials and sitcoms. Representatives will be at the Wilmington Hilton, Sunday from 12 noon—5 PM. Complimentary evaluations and testing. Training available.*"

"Modeling/Acting Jobs. TV, fashion, photo, films. Regional work."

"Modeling: Gorgeous! All types for national TV commercials and modeling. Call immediately."

"Models/Actors. New entertainment company needs professional DJ's, exotic dancers (M/F), playboy bunnies, Chippendale's, for balloon deliveries. Make top $$."

"Models, Actors, Talent wanted—New York Modeling Convention. Audition for over 100 agents, casting directors, producers. Waldorf Astoria Hotel."

SAG office: none.

Film Commission: Carol Myers, Director. Delaware Development Office 99 Kings Highway, P.O. Box 1401, Dover, Delaware 19903; 302-739-4271; 800-441-8846; FAX 302-739-5749.

Department of Administrative Services/Division of Business and Occupational Regulation: 302-739-4522

DISTRICT OF COLUMBIA (Washington, D.C.)
Does the District of Columbia have a problem with entertainment scams? No.

Licensing: The District of Columbia does not have specific laws regulating talent/modeling agencies. Employment agencies must be licensed by the Mayor's office and the Department of Consumer and Regulatory Affairs. A written examination is required. A bond is required by the District of Columbia in the amount of $5,000. An additional bond may be required by the Mayor's office.

Newspaper: The Washington Post

Published Disclaimer: None.

Sample Ads:
"MODEL SEARCH...Beginners & professionals. Local
office of top international agency seeks new faces. We
need guys and girls, large or small, petite or tall.
Training available. Call: John Casablancas Model and
Talent Management."

"The 1993 International Cover Model Search! Our
discoveries are in Vogue, Cosmo, Glamour, Bazaar, Teen,
Elle, Seventeen, etc. Call M-F, 11-6, for information.
Open call Saturday, 11:00-4:30."

"Model Search—We are looking for new faces, see our
ad. John Casablancas Model & Talent Mgmt."

SAG Office: 5480 Wisconsin Avenue, Suite 201, Chevy Chase,
Maryland 20815, 301-657-2560.

Film Commission: Crystal Palmer Brazil, Director. Mayor's
Office of TV & Film 717 14th Street NW, 10th Fl., Washington,
DC, 20005; Tel 202-727-6600; FAX 202-727-3787.

Department of Consumer and Regulatory Affairs: 202-727-7989

FLORIDA
Does Florida have problems with entertainment scams? No.

Licensing: Florida has specific laws which apply to "talent
agencies." Talent agencies require a license from the Department
of Professional Regulation. Agency owners are fingerprinted and
photographed, for examination by the police. Agency owners
must prove at least one year similar experience.

Agencies cannot require subscription to a publication, post
card service, advertisement, resume service, photographer,
school, acting school, workshop, acting workshop, video or audio tapes. All advertising must contain the name of the agency,
address, license number and the words "talent agency."

Agencies must pay talent five days after receiving payment
from the client. Agencies must provide talent with specific and
detailed employment contracts. Any collected fees or expenses

must be returned by the agency within 48 hours, if no employment was procured. Agencies must maintain a permanent office and regular business hours. A bond is required in the amount of $5,000.

Newspaper: The Miami Herald

Published Disclaimer: None.

Sample Ads: "Model and Talent Agencies" and "Models/ Promo/ Shows/Photo"are listings in the employment index, but no such ads were found in this sample. The following "model" ads did appear:
   "Elite Models, Private dancing 24 hours."

   "Model outcall dancers—Private sessions."

SAG Office: 7300 North Kendall Drive, Suite 620, Miami, 33156, 305-670-7677.

Film Commission: John Reitzammer, Director, Florida Entertainment Commission, 112 West Adams Street, Suite 100, Jacksonville, Florida 32202; 904-798-4300, 818-777-1613 (California office); FAX 904-798-4303

Department of Professional Regulation and Complaints: 904-922-4977

GEORGIA
Does Georgia have a problem with entertainment scams? Yes.

How are problems solved: Education efforts; Attorney General and Consumer Affairs. The film commission conducts undercover investigations.

Licensing: Georgia does not have state laws regulating employment agencies (which includes talent/modeling agencies).

Newspaper: The Atlanta Journal-Constitution

   Published Disclaimer: "We reserve the right to censor, reclassify, revise, edit, or reject any classified advertisement not meeting our standards for acceptance."

   Also:

   Sample Ads:

   "Hollywood in Atlanta. Want to be in film/tv? We book talent most everyday, right here in Atlanta. Phone for interview."

   "Actors/Actresses. No experience necessary. We are booking talent for film/tv most everyday. Male/female, most ages. You do not need photos or training for interview. The William Reynolds Agency. 14 years in Atlanta."

   "Actor/Actress. If you can handle small speaking parts in movies & tv making up to $1,000/day, phone for your FREE SCREEN TEST. You may qualify for our proven success program. No experience needed. MBA Screen Actors Group, Inc."

   "Act/Models. If selected, get FREE PHOTO SESSION and roll of film via portfolio. Beginners okay. R&M Production."

   "Actors/Models. $125/hr. (salary). Nat'l magazine, major motion pictures. All types, ages, beginners okay, immediately. Allied Artist."

   "Actors/Models. $135/hr. Booking now. TV,

commercials, movies, nat'l magazines. All ages/types. Beginners okay."

"Model/Actor. All ages! All types! Atlanta Book of General Models is looking for new faces to market for upcoming projects. TV–Film–Print–Catalogue."

"Model Search. All ages, beginners okay. $50-$150. JLH Enterprises."

SAG Office: 455 East Paces Ferry Road NE, Suite 334, Atlanta, Georgia, 30305; 404-239-0131

Film Commission: Norman Bielowicz, Director. Georgia Film & Videotape Office, 285 Peachtree Center Avenue, Suite 1000, Atlanta, Georgia 30301, 404-656-3591; FAX 404-651-9063.

Regulatory Association: Georgia Association of Personnel Services (G.A.P.S.): 404-255-9157

HAWAII

Does Hawaii have a problem with entertainment scams? No.

How problems are solved: Not applicable.

Licensing: Hawaii does not have specific laws regulating talent/modeling agencies. Employment agencies must be licensed by the Department of Commerce and Consumer Affairs. Employment agents must pass a "certified employment consultant" examination. Employment contracts must be specific and detailed. No employment agency can require talent to sign over power-of-attorney. Employment agencies must include its company name in all advertising. Employment agencies cannot collect an advance registration fee. A bond is required in the amount of $5,000.

Newspaper: The Honolulu Advertiser and Star-Bulletin

Published disclaimer: "All ads are subject to approval before publication. We reserve the right to edit, refuse, reject or cancel any ad at any time." And: "Advertising Standards: Advertising published in *The Honolulu Advertiser* and *Star-Bulletin* is accepted on the premise that the merchandise and/or services offered are accurately described and willingly sold to customers at the advertised price. Advertisers are aware of these conditions. Advertising that does not conform to these standards or that is deceptive or misleading is never knowingly accepted. If any reader encounters noncompliance with these standards, we ask that you inform Classified Advertising, or Better Business Bureau."

Sample Ads: none found.

SAG office: 949 Kapiolani Blvd. Suite 105, Honolulu, Hawaii; 96814, 808-596-0388

Film Commission: Georgette Deemer, Director. Hawaii Film Office P.O. Box 2359, Honolulu, Hawaii 96804; 808-586-2570; FAX 808-586-2572.

Department of Commerce and Consumer Affairs/Employment Agency Regulation: 808-586-3000

IDAHO
Does Idaho have problems with entertainment scams? Yes.

How problems are solved: The film commission becomes involved in any complaints.

Licensing: Idaho does not have state laws which regulate employment agencies (which includes talent/modeling agencies).

Newspaper: The Idaho Statesman

Published Disclaimers:

> **WARNING**
> The Idaho Statesman recommends that you investigate every phase of investment opportunities, especially those from out of state or offered by a person doing business out of a local motel or hotel.
>
> Investment offerings must be registered with the Idaho Department of Finance.
>
> We suggest you consult your attorney, the Better Business Bureau, Idaho Department of Finance, or the Idaho Consumer Affairs office.

Sample Ads: None found.

SAG office: none.

Film Commission: Peg Owens Crist, Director. Idaho Film Bureau 700 West State St., 2nd Floor., Boise, Idaho 83720; 208-334-2470; 800-942-8338; FAX 208-334-2631

Regulatory Agency: Not applicable.

ILLINOIS

Does Illinois have problems with entertainment scams? Yes.

How problems are solved: Attorney General. The State places advertisements in local entertainment newspapers, interacts with licensesd agents and, distributes printed cautions to talent and models.

Licensing: Illinois has laws which specifically apply to "Theatrical employment agencies." An agency can only charge a maximum $4 registration fee, and only if granted such a permit. This fee is subject to return on demand if no position is procured. Agents cannot require a subscription to a publication, post card service or advertisement. Agents must send out "referral slips" with each job. Agents cannot have a prison record nor belong to

"subversive societies." Agencies cannot advertise without a bona
fide job order. Also, theatrical employment agencies must provide talent with detailed and specific employment contracts. Theatrical employment agencies must be bonded in the amount of
$5,000.

Newspaper: Chicago Tribune

Published Disclaimer: none

Sample Ads:
"*Models/Talent. . . Due to rapid growth, we're looking
for new faces for local and national exposure. Male or
female, all ages, experienced, or inexperienced. You don't
need schooling. It's never too late to get started. Flexible
hours. Fashion shows, promotional, tv, film,
photography. For appointment call. . . licensed and
bonded. "*

"*Actors all professional hotline. Never a charge.*"

"*International Model and Talent Search. . . models,
actors, singers, dancers. Ages 4—90. Grand Prize
finalists will receive trip to California to meet hundreds
of worldwide contract awarding agents. Other prizes
awarded. We offer support to every contestant. Call now
to audition.*"

"*Models, actors, real people. We need new faces. All
types and ages.*"

"*Modeling. Let John Casablanca's take your picture and
show it to the world. Call for more information.*"

SAG office: 307 N. Michigan Ave., Chicago, IL 60601, 312-
372-8081.

Film Commission: Suzy Kellett, Director. Illinois Film Office
100 West Randolph, Suite 3-400, Chicago, Illinois 60601; 312-814-
3600; FAX 312-814-6732.

Department of Labor/Employment Agencies: 312/793-2810

INDIANA

Does Indiana have a problem with entertainment scams? Not wide-spread.

How problems are solved: The film office will alert the community of possible problems and legal action will be taken, if necessary.

Licensing: Indiana does not have specific laws regulating talent/modeling agencies. Employment agencies must be licensed by the Department of Revenue. An employment agency is any person who by using cards, circulars, pamphlets or any other advertising offers to secure employment. Employment agencies must provide detailed and specific employment contracts. A bond is required in the amount of $1,000.

Newspaper: The Indianapolis Star

Published Disclaimer: "We reserve the right to edit, properly classify, cancel or decline any ad. We will not knowingly accept advertising that discriminates on the basis of sex, age, religion, race, national origin or physical disability. No position guarantees can be given."

Sample ads:

> *"Models/Talent. . . Kristie of Chicago, Indianapolis branch. Due to rapid growth, we're looking for new faces for local and national exposure. Male or female, all ages, experienced or inexperienced. You don't need schooling. It's never too late to get started. Flexible hours. Fashion shows, promotions, TV, film, photography. For appointment call...Licensed and bonded."*

SAG Office: None

Film Commission: Jane Roulon, Director, Indiana Tourism & Film Development Division/Department of Commerce, 1 North Capitol, Suite 700, Indianapolis, Indiana 46204, Tel 317-232-8829; FAX 317-233-6887.

Department of Revenue: 317-232-4216

IOWA

Does Iowa have a problem with entertainment scams? Yes.

How problems are solved: Public awareness efforts.

Licensing: Iowa does not have specific laws regulating talent/modeling agencies. Employment agencies are licensed by the Division of Labor. No fees "or other thing of value in excess of one dollar" can be collected in advance by employment agencies. Employment agencies cannot collect more than a 15% commission of talent's gross earnings. Employment contracts must stipulate if the job is a form of "entertainment enterprise" (i.e., circus, vaudeville, theatrical or stage). Employment agencies must provide detailed and specific contracts. A bond is required in the amount of $20,000.

Newspaper: The Des Moines Register

Published disclaimer: "To serve our customers well, *The Register* will properly classify all ads and may edit to ensure good results and reflect accepted standards of taste. We do not knowingly accept ads that violate the law and assume all real estate, employment, merchandise and services are available on an equal opportunity basis. *The Register* reserves the right to classify, edit, reject or cancel any ad at any time."

SAG office: none.

Film Commission: Wendol Jarvis, Director. Iowa Film Office/ Department of Economic Development, 200 E. Grand Ave., Des Moines, Iowa 50309, Tel 515-242-4726; 800-779-3456; FAX 515-242-4859.

Division of Labor: 515-281-8067

KANSAS
Does Kansas have a problem with entertainment scams? No.

Licensing: Kansas does not have specific laws regulating talent/modeling agencies. Employment agencies must be licensed by the Department of Human Resources. Employment agencies cannot charge a registration fee of more than $2. If no employment is secured within three days, all registration fees must be returned on demand. A bond is required in the amount of $500.

Newspaper: The Kansas City Star

Published disclaimer: "The *Star* may, in its sole discretion, edit, classify or reject any advertising copy."

Sample ads:

> *"Actors & other artsy types. We need energetic individuals to help sell the seats for the Lyric Opera..."*

> *"Actors/Models. Professional. $75-$95/hr. and TV, film extras $75-$225/day. No experience required. 10 years in business."*

> *"Models/Dancers needed. Top pay, flexible hours."*

SAG Office: none.

Film Commission: Vicky Henley, Director. Kansas Film Commission 700 SW Harrison St.,Suite 1300, Topeka, Kansas 66603; 913-296-4927; FAX 913-296-6988.

Department of Human Resources: 913-296-4062

KENTUCKY
Does Kentucky have a problem with entertainment scams? Yes.

How problems are solved: Public Protection Agency and Attorney General.

Licensing: Kentucky does not have specific laws regulating talent/modeling agencies. Employment agencies must be licensed by the Cabinet for Human Resources. Employment agencies cannot charge or collect advance registration fees. Employment agencies cannot require talent to subscribe to any publications or "incidental service or contribute to the cost of advertising." Employment agencies cannot advertise for positions unless the positions exist. The agency name must appear in all advertising. A bond is required in the amount of $5,000.

Newspaper: The Lexington Herald-Leader

Published disclaimer: none.

Sample ads: none found.

SAG office: none.

Film Commission: Russ Slone, Manager, Kentucky Film Office, 500 Mero St., Capitol Plaza Tower, 22nd Fl., Frankfort, Kentucky 40601; 502-564-3456; 800-345-6591; FAX 502-564-7588.

Cabinet for Human Resources: 502-564-3296

LOUISIANA
Does Louisiana have a problem with entertainment scams? Yes.

How problems are solved: Public awareness efforts. The film commission will involve the media and police, if necessary.

Licensing: Louisiana does not have specific laws regulating talent/modeling agencies. Employment agencies must be licensed by the Department of Employment. Employment agencies may charge a $10 fee for the preparation of a job resume, but cannot charge an advance registration fee.

Employment agencies cannot require talent to subscribe to publications, or photographic service, postal card service, or letter service or to contribute to the cost of advertising. Talent must receive a copy of every employment contract, which must be detailed and specific. Agencies cannot ask talent to sign over power-of-attorney. Owners, operators and managers of agencies are required to take a written examination administered by the Department of Employment. Agency owners must submit a resume detailing their business involvements for the last ten years. Agents are prohibited from interviewing talent in private residences. All advertising must contain the name of the agency. Employment agencies cannot legally charge more than a 15% commission. A bond is required in the amount of $5,000.

Newspaper: The Times-Picayune

Published disclaimer: None.

Sample Ads: None found.

SAG office: none.

Film Commission: David Jones, Director. Louisiana Film Commission P.O. Box 44320, Baton Rouge, Louisiana 70804-4320, 504-342-8150; FAX 504-342-7988.

Department of Employment and Training/Office of Labor: 504-342-7691

MAINE
Does Maine have a problem with entertainment scams? No.

Licensing: Maine does not have state laws regulating employment agencies (which includes talent/modeling agencies).

Newspaper: The Bangor Daily News

Published Disclaimer: none.

Sample Ads: none found.

Newspaper: The Maine Telegram

Published Disclaimer: none.

Sample Ads: none found.

SAG Office: none.

Film Commission: D. Lea Girardin, Director, Maine Film Office, State House, Station 59, Augusta, Maine 04333; 207-287-5707; FAX 207-287-5701.

Regulatory agency: Not applicable.

MARYLAND
Does Maryland have a problem with entertainment scams? Yes.

How problems are solved: Networking with licensing authorities and educational efforts.

Licensing: Maryland has specific laws which regulate "theatrical employment agencies." Theatrical employment agencies must be licensed as employment agencies. Employment agencies are licensed by the Division of Labor and Industry. All advertising must contain the agency name. Agencies are allowed a maximum 20% commission on temporary placement. Agencies can only advertise for bona fide positions. Agencies cannot charge advance registration fees. A bond is required in the amount of $7,000.

Newspaper: The Baltimore Sun

Published Disclaimer: none.

Sample Ads:
"Modeling—'Fresh Faces' for east and west coast
clients. Possible posters, movies and commercials. Long
hair OK. No experience required. 4 years and older."

"Model/Actor search. Casting all types 3 TV shows, 3
films, 4 commercials, photos. Full service, excellent pay.
Part-time immediate work. Screen test."

SAG office: The Highland House, 5480 Wisconsin Ave. Suite 201, Chevy Chase, Maryland, 20815, 301-657-2560

Film Commission: Michael Styler, Director. Maryland Film Commission 601 North Howard Street, Baltimore, Maryland 21201; 410-333-6633; FAX 410-333-1062.

Department of Licensing and Regulation/Division of Labor and Industry: 410-333-4211

MASSACHUSETTS
Does Massachusetts have problems with entertainment scams? No.

Licensing: Massachusetts has laws which specifically apply to theatrical agents, booking agents, personal agents modeling agencies and actor's managers. Any person who is a theatrical agent must obtain a license from the Public Safety Commission. Agencies which employ models must obtain a license from the Department of Labor. Agents must provide talent with detailed and specific employment contracts. An agent's commission cannot result in talent receiving less than state or Federal minimum wage.

Agents cannot require talent to buy subscriptions or contribute to advertising. Agencies cannot charge advance registration fees. Agencies cannot advertise without the agency name, address and identification as an agency in the ad.

Agencies cannot send "any female to any place which the employment agency knows or should have known permits persons known to be prostitutes, gamblers or procurers or intoxicated persons to frequent such place."

Theatrical booking agencies must be bonded by the Public Safety Commission in the amount of $1,000. Modeling agencies must be bonded by the Department of Labor in the amount of $3,000.

Newspaper: Boston Globe

Published Disclaimer: none.

Sample Ad: none found.

SAG Office: 11 Beacon Street, Suite 505, Boston, Massachusetts 02108; 617-742-2688

Film Commission: Linda Peterson Warren, Director. Massachusetts Film Office 10 Park Plaza, Suite 2310, Boston, Massachusetts 02116, Tel 617-973-8800; FAX 617-973-8810.

Department of Labor and Industries: 617-727-3696

MICHIGAN
Does Michigan have problems with entertainment scams? No.

Licensing: In November 1992, the state of Michigan repealed a 13 year-old law which specifically applied to "Theatrical employment agencies." The reason the law was repealed was reportedly because "there were no complaints." Michigan presently has no laws which regulate the employment of actors, performers, models or entertainers.

Newspaper: Detroit Free Press

Published Disclaimer: None

Sample Ad:

"Models. . . 2 years through adult. Selecting new faces for promotion to local and major advertisers/commercial producers. No experience necessary. Presentations at: 5 PM or 7 PM sharp on Sunday at Troy Marriott. Minors must be with legal guardian. PA/NYC."

SAG office: 28690 Southfield Road., Lathrup Village, Michigan 48076; 810-559-9540

Film Commission: Janet Lockwood, Director. Michigan Film Office 525 West Ottawa, P.O. Box 30004, Lansing, Michigan 48909; 517-373-0638; 800-477-FILM; FAX 517-373-3872.

Department of Commerce/Bureau of Occupational and Professional Regulation: 517-373-1870, 517-373-1654

MINNESOTA

Does Minnesota have a problem with entertainment scams: No.

Licensing: Minnesota has specific laws regulating "Entertainment agencies." Entertainment agencies must be licensed by the Department of Labor. Two reputable character references, who will "provide an insight into the applicant's character and demeanor," are required for licensing. A bond is required in the amount of $10,000.

Newspaper: The Star-Tribune

Published Disclaimer: "All ad copy must be approved by the newspaper, which reserves the right to request changes, reject, or properly classify an ad. The advertiser, and not the newspaper, is responsible for the truthful content of the ad."

Sample Ads:
"*Open Audition. Head Bookers and Scouts from Michelle Pommier models of Miami and Rare Models of Minneapolis will be auditioning print, runway and fashion models for Minneapolis, Miami, New York, Los Angeles, Paris, Italy, London, Spain, Australia, Japan, Greece, Germany.*"

"*Mystery Cafe. Auditioning experienced actor/actresses only please. For immediate and other positions. Good pay.*"

"*Contestants Wanted. Interested in horses and rodeo? Compete for the coveted title of Miss Rodeo Minnesota.*"

"*Caryn's—Winner of '92 Int'l Model and Talent School of the Year Award. Looking for new faces.*"

"*Acting for non-actors. Skill, fun, personal growth. The Acting Studio.*"

"Models Wanted. Complimentary auditions to train for commercials, photography, tv, fashion shows and promotions. John Casablanca's Modeling Center."

SAG Office: 708 East First Street, Minneapolis, Minnesota 55402, 612-371-9120.

Film Commission: Randy Adamsick and Kelly Pratt, Co-Directors, Minnesota Film Board, 401 North 3rd Street, Suite 401, Minneapolis, Minnesota 55401; 612-332-6493, FAX 612-332-3735.

Department of Labor and Industry: 612-296-2282

MISSISSIPPI
Does Mississippi have a problem with entertainment scams? Yes.

How problems are solved: Refers to proper regulatory agency.

Licensing: Mississippi does not have specific laws regulating employment agencies (which includes talent/modeling agencies). The only talent agency listed in the state has a city business license and charges the state allowable maximum 15% commission for employment in commercials and a 10% commission for employment in feature films. This talent agency claimed that the state wanted to classify her business as a "Junior College." The amount of bond required may soon increase from $10,000 to $50,000.

Newspaper:
The Clarion Ledger

Published Disclaimer:
None.

Sample Ad: (see right)

SAG Office: none.

Film Commission: Ward Emling, Director. Mississippi Film Office 1200 Walter Sillers Bldg., P.O. Box 849, Jackson, Mississippi 39205; 601-359-3297; FAX 601-359-5757.

Regulatory agency: Not applicable.

MISSOURI
Does Missouri have a problem with entertainment scams? No.

Licensing: Missouri has specific laws regulating "theatrical booking agencies." Theatrical booking agencies must be licensed as employment agencies. Employment agencies must be licensed by the Department of Labor. Employment agencies that charge registration fees, must return all fees in full upon demand, if employment is not procured within one month after registration.

Employment agencies cannot send "any female applying for employment to any house of prostitution...or other immoral resort."

A bond in the amount of $500 is required.

Newspaper: The St. Louis Post-Dispatch

Published Disclaimer: "Before responding to any advertisement requesting that money be sent or invested, you may wish to investigate the company and offering. *The St. Louis Post-Dispatch* cannot assume any responsibility for the validity of the offerings advertised within the classified pages. For more information and assistance regarding the investigation of Business Opportunities, the *St. Louis Post-Dispatch* urges its readers to contact the Better Business Bureau."

Sample Ads:
"Model Auditions. Interviewing all ages for commercials, ads, and fashion shows. Beginners/ Experienced considered."

"Models—All Ages/Sizes. Start Fall with new exciting career. Earn $$$."

"Models. Fall fashion shows, promos and TV commercials. Call for audition."

"Models for ladies lingerie shows and printwork."

"Models 18 and over for glamour/lady's lingerie."

SAG Office: 906 Olive Street, Suite 1006, St. Louis, Missouri 63101, 314-231-8410.

Film Commission: Kate Arnold-Schuck, Director. Missouri Film Commission P.O. Box 1055, 301 W. High, Jefferson City, Missouri 65102; 314-751-9050, FAX 314-751-5160.

Department of Labor and Industrial Relations/Division of Labor Standards: 314-751-3403

MONTANA

Does Montana have a problem with entertainment scams? Yes.

How problems are solved: Problems are solved firsthand by the film commission, with municipal assistance, public awareness efforts, and media cooperation.

Licensing: Montana does not have specific laws regulating talent/modeling agencies. Employment agencies must be licensed by the Department of Commerce. Employment agencies must provide detailed and specific contracts. Agencies cannot charge or accept advance registration or application fees. The symbol "$$$" cannot be used in advertising as a substitute for salary range. Employment agencies cannot advertise as being "licensed" unless they identify by whom. A bond in the amount of $2,000 is required. Montana does have a state Private Employment Agency Association.

Newspaper: The Billings Gazette

Published Disclaimer: none

Sample Ads: none

SAG Office: None

Film Commission: Lonie Stimac, Director. Montana Film Office 1424 9th Ave., Helena, Montana 59620; 406-444-2654, 800-553-4563, FAX 406-444-1800.

Department of Commerce: 406-444-3797

NEBRASKA

Does Nebraska have a problem with entertainment scams? No.

Licensing: Nebraska does not have specific laws which regulate talent/modeling agencies. Employment agencies must be licensed by the Department of Labor. Employment agencies must retain copies of all advertisements. Detailed and specific contracts must be provided to talent and the Labor Department. Employment agencies cannot charge a fee more than $5 for advertising or reference checks, nor require talent to subscribe to any publication. A bond is required in the amount of $10,000.

Newspaper: The Lincoln Journal-Star

Published Disclaimer: "The *Journal-Star* may, in its sole discretion, edit, classify or reject any advertising copy."

Sample Ads: none

SAG Office: None:

Film Commission: Mary Ethel Emanuel, Acting Director, Nebraska Film Office, P.O. Box 94666, 700 South 16th Street, Lincoln, Nebraska, 68509; 402-471-3797, 800-228-4307, FAX 402-471-3026.

Department of Labor: Raymond Griffin 402-595-3095

NEVADA
Does Nevada have a problem with entertainment scams? Yes.

> *February 28, 1992:*The Hollywood Reporter *headline read "Rape Suspect Tells Victims He's Producer." William John Wood (aka "Max Carson") is wanted by the FBI on charges of kidnapping and sexual assault and battery on an aspiring actress. She was lured by Carson to a motel room for a commercial he was producing and was attacked by him.*

> *April 29, 1992:*Las Vegas police arrested a 52 year-old man in the 1987 murder of a teenage girl found floating in the Colorado River. Thomas Preston befriended the 17 year-old girl under the ruse he was a talent agent. Preston was apprehended in South Dakota.*

How problems are solved: The Film Office involves the media and licensing and enforcement authorities at all government levels. Public awareness efforts include statewide workshops and printed cautions to talent and models. Televisedpublic service announcements feature warnings from the Attorney General and Lieutenan Governor.

Licensing: Nevada does not have specific laws which regulate talent/modeling agencies. Employment agencies must be licensed by the Labor Commission. The commission on gross wage for jobs which last over a month cannot exceed 65%, and cannot exceed 40% on jobs which last seven or more days but less than 30 days. The lawful maximum allowable talent agency commission for talent or modeling jobs which last less than a week is 0%, though an unwritten maximum of 40% is allowed.

Employment agencies cannot charge "fees of any kind for the registration of applicants," or subscription to a publication, or as a contribution to advertising. Employment agencies cannot conduct business in, "a room used for sleeping or as a residence." All advertising must contain the name and address of the agency.

Any individual or company that implies the possibility of employment, must be licensed by the State Labor Commission. A bond is required in the amount of $1,000.

Newspaper: The Las Vegas Review–Journal/Sun

Published Disclaimer: "The *Las Vegas Review-Journal/Sun* do not vouch for the legitimacy of items, jobs, or money making opportunities advertised in this classification. We suggest you carefully evaluate such offers and not send money to these advertisers unless you are certain you know with whom you are dealing and you know all terms and conditions of the offer."

Also:

"The *Review-Journal/Sun* reserve the right to edit, reject, or revise all copy to conform to policy and/or correct classification." The following Notice is published (depending on the newspaper) in statewide newspapers: "Actors/Actresses. Notice to talent and models. If you have any questions regarding the legitimacy of a talent agent, producer, casting director, personal manager, modeling school, fashion photographer, or related area, check with the State Motion Picture Division."

Sample Ads:
"Models, Young and attractive ladies needed for new Penthouse type magazine. Modeling experience is NOT required."

"Actor/Actress. Film Producer will finance and develop film talent. Send photo."

"Actress—Adult Telephone. F/T or P/T. Must be able to work a variety of shifts. Legal, licensed, ethical adult business."

"Models, 1992 Int'l Cover Model Search. Top fashion magazines, tv, film."

> *"Models/Model Types. Perfume promoting, local department stores."*

> "Models needed immediately for over 20 upcoming catalog and magazine projects. No experience necessary. Male/Female. 5'2"—6'2". Send photo and address to Beverly Hills, CA... "

SAG Office: 2905 King Midas Way, Las Vegas, Nevada 89102, 702-364-0803.

Film Commission: Bob Hirsch, Director, Nevada Motion Picture Division/Commission on Economic Development, 3770 Howard Hughes Pkwy., Suite 295, Las Vegas, Nevada 89109; 702-486-7150, FAX 702-486-7372.

Labor Commission: 702-687-4850

NEW HAMPSHIRE
Does New Hampshire have a problem with entertainment scams? No.

Licensing: New Hampshire does not have state laws regulating employment agencies (which includes talent/modeling agencies).

Newspaper: The Manchester Union

Published Disclaimer: none.

Sample Ads: none found.

SAG office: none.

Film Commission: No state funded Film Commission. Contact: Ann Kennard, New Hampshire Tourism/Film & TV Bureau 172 Pembroke Rd., P.O. Box 1856, Concord, New Hampshire, 03302-1856; 603-271-2598, ext. 108, FAX 603-271-2629.

Regulatory agency: Not applicable.

NEW JERSEY

Does New Jersey have a problem with entertainment scams? Yes.

How problems are solved: Attorney General's modeling and theatrical agency task force.

Licensing: New Jersey has specific laws regulating "booking agencies." Booking agencies are classified as employment agencies, which are licensed by the Bureau of Employment & Personnel Services. An agency cannot conduct business in a residence, unless separate exits and entrances are provided. Agents cannot operate out of premises rented or leased on an hourly, daily, weekly or other "transient basis." Agents cannot accept fees for "a service rendered or product sold" when no employment has been accepted. All advertising must contain the name and address of the agency. A bond is required in the amount of $10,000.

Newspaper: The Star-Ledger

Published Disclaimer: none.

Sample Ads: "
Actors TV, commercials, film. No experience OK."

"Model/Actors. Movie Extras. All types wanted. No experience required. Now working on NEW COSBY TV SHOW. Kids-seniors for commercials. Adults-teens extra work. Over 6,000 already worked. USA Extras/ Casting #BWO136901."

"Models Needed. Children 6 mos.-16 yrs. No experience necessary. No portfolios or schooling required. Immediate assignments if qualified. $75/$150 per hour. Reid Elliot Management Group #BWO283200."

"Models/Actors—All ages. NJ's 'Action' Talent Agent. Now submitting for: Elton John video, 'Gone With the Wind' tv mini-series. Our experience and contacts guarantee weekly opportunities in TV, movie, video,

print. Free expert training for beginners. No fee. Bonded. Lic. #BWO284000. Clifton, NJ."

"Models. Voice-over people needed immediately. All voices, all types. No experience necessary."

SAG office: none.

Film Commission: Joseph Friedman, Director, New Jersey Motion Picture & Television Commission, P.O. Box 47023, 153 Halsey St., Newark, New Jersey 07101; 201-648-6279, FAX 201-648-7350.

Bureau of Employment and Personnel Services/Consumer Affairs: 201-504-6367

NEW MEXICO
Does New Mexico have a problem with entertainment scams? Yes.

How are problems solved: Public awareness efforts.

Licensing: New Mexico does not have laws regulating employment agencies (which includes talent/modeling agencies). A booklet published by the State Department of Labor, "How the New Mexico State Labor Law Protects You," covers this state's labor regulations.

Newspaper: The Albuquerque Journal

Published Disclaimer: "The publisher reserves the right to properly classify, edit, revise, or reject any and all advertising."

Sample Ads: none

SAG Office: none.

Film Commission: Linda Taylor-Hutchison, Director. New Mexico Film Commission 1050 Pecos Trail, Sante Fe, New Mexico 87501; 505-827-7365; 800-545-9871; FAX 505-827-7369.

Department of Labor/Labor and Industrial Division: 505-827-6875

NEW YORK

Does New York have a problem with entertainment scams? Yes.

How are problems solved: Attorney General, Consumer Affairs. The state Attorney General and local AFTRA office print and distribute a joint brochure entitled, *"Do You Want To Be An Actor, Announcer or a Model?"*

Licensing: New York has specific laws regulating "Theatrical agencies." Theatrical agencies (which includes talent/modeling) are licensed as employment agencies. Employment agencies must be licensed by the Department of Labor. (The New York City Department of Consumer Affairs regulates employment agencies under the same laws). Applicants for licenses must be fingerprinted. Agencies cannot operate from residences. Agencies must provide detailed and specific job contracts.

Advance registration fees are unlawful. Agency commissions cannot exceed 10%. All advertisements must contain the agency name, address, and the word, "agency." Agencies cannot require subscription to a publication or require talent to contribute to advertising. Agencies cannot refuse "to return on demand of an applicant any baggage or personal property belonging to such applicant." A bond is required in the amount of $5,000.

Newspaper: The New York Times

Published Disclaimer: none.

Sample Ads: none found.

SAG Office: 1515 Broadway, 44th Floor, New York, New York 10036, 212-944-1030.

Film Commission: Bruce Feinberg, Director, New York State Governor's Office for Motion Picture/TV Development, Pier 62, West 23rd St. & Hudson River, Suite 307, New York, New York 10011; 212-929-0240; FAX 212-929-0506.

Department of Labor: 718-797-7398

NORTH CAROLINA
Does North Carolina have problems with entertainment scams?
No.

Licensing: North Carolina does not have laws regulating talent/modeling agencies. The Department of Labor licenses, "Private personnel services." Advance placement fees or registration fees are prohibited. Agency owners are investigated for criminal record, business integrity and character. Advertising must include the name of the private personnel service and the words, "personnel service." A fee "may be charged for resume writing." A bond is required in the amount of $10,000. There is a Private Personnel Service Advisory Council.

Newspaper: The Raleigh News and Observer

Published Disclaimer: "We make every effort to print only those ads deemed credible. We reserve the right to revise, edit or reject any or all copy. Please submit a letter to the Classified Director any time the offer implied differs from the actual offer. Address: Classified Director, *The News and Observer*, P.O. Box 191, Raleigh, NC 27602."

Sample Ads: None

SAG Office: None.

Film Commission: William Arnold, Director, North Carolina Film Commission, 420 N. Salisbury St., Raleigh, North Carolina 27611; 919-733-9900; FAX 919-715-0151.

Department of Labor/Private Personnel Service Division: 919-733-7166

NORTH DAKOTA
Does North Dakota have a problem with entertainment scams?
No.

Licensing: North Dakota has specific laws regulating, "Theatrical agencies." Theatrical agencies are licensed as employment agencies. Employment agencies must be licensed by the Labor Department. Agencies must provide talent with detailed and specific job contracts. Agencies cannot accept advance registration fees. A bond is required in the amount of $5,000.

Newspaper: The Bismark Tribune

Published Disclaimer: None.

Sample Ads:
"Models Wanted. All types, no experience. For catalogs and upcoming magazine ads. Earn $100/ hr. or more. For more information. See our fashion ad in Glamour's June issue."

SAG Office: None
Film Commission: Jeff Eslinger, Director, North Dakota Film Commission, 604 East Boulevard, 2nd Floor, Bismarck, North Dakota 58505; 701-224-2525; 800-435-5663; FAX 701-224-4878.

Department of Labor: 701-224-2660

OHIO
Does Ohio have problems with entertainment scams? Yes.

How are problems solved: Education efforts; Attorney General, if necessary.

Licensing: Ohio does not have specific laws regulating talent/modeling agencies. "Personnel Placement Services" must be licensed by the Department of Commerce. There is no bond required.

Newspaper: The Plain Dealer

Published Disclaimer: None.

Sample Ads:

"Interested in Modeling? John Casablanca's Modeling Center will be bringing in the talent scout from American Models of New York, at the Radisson Hotel. Males/Females, experienced or not, training available, 12 years on up. Call for details. Reg. #89-11-1238M."

"A Star Search. Children/Teens. Powers Int'l, on behalf of Wilhelmina Models, is looking for children and teens to enter Kid Search '92. If you have a child or teen, 4 years to 17 years of age, consider this chance of a lifetime. For a FREE appointment, please forward a photo (nonreturnable) with name, age and phone number to Powers Int'l/WWM Search."

"Actors/Audition. L.A. Opportunity. Dynasty, Medical Center, Trapper John M.D., Vegas, Houston Nights, L.A. Law and Aaron Spelling Productions represent just a few credits to the name of Gary Shaffer (Casting Director) and Lawrence Folgo (Producer). They will choose 2 actors to participate in a very exciting program with Hollywood casting opportunities. Must be available to be in L.A. for at LEAST 3 months. . . Must be 18 or over. Must be willing to seek sponsorship for expenses. Call the American Performing Arts Network for your appointment to screen test." (See "It Can Happen To You" section, June 17, 1993, Jenny Jones .")

"Full figure females. Thinking of getting into the exciting world of modeling? YOU CAN DO IT. . . BUT GET THE FACTS FIRST! Dolores Presley of Dimensions Plus Size Agency will be screening potential models, ages 16 and up, sizes 12/over, to work with her very lucrative agency. There is a growing market for PLUS

*models. We need you NOW. No previous experience
necessary. Call the American Performing Arts Network
for your qualification interview.*"

SAG Office: 1367 E. 6th Street, Suite 229, Cleveland, Ohio 44114;
216-579-9305.

Film Commission: Eve Lapolla, Director. Ohio Film Bureau
77 S. High St., 29th Fl., P.O. Box 1001, Columbus, Ohio 43266-
0101; 614-466-2284; 800-848-1300; FAX 614-466-6744.

Department of Commerce: 614-466-4130

OKLAHOMA
Does Oklahoma have a problem with entertainment scams? Yes.

How are problems solved: Educational efforts, media cooperation. The film commission investigates suspicious activities
and will involve the police if necessary.

Licensing: Oklahoma does not have specific laws regulating talent/modeling agencies. Employment agencies must be licensed by the Department of Labor. Applicants for employment
agency licenses must prove at least one year prior experience as
an agent and provide three personal references. Agents are allowed a 15% maximum commission. Advance registration fees
are prohibited. All advertising must contain the agency name
and address. A bond is required in the amount of $5,000.

Newspaper: The Oklahoman

Published Disclaimer: "These newspapers reserve the right
to reject, edit, revise, and properly classify all advertising submitted for publication. The publisher also reserves the right to
cancel any advertisement at any time."

Sample Ads:
*"Models wanted. Complimentary auditions to train for
commercials, photography, tv, fashion shows and*

promotions. John Casablanca's Modeling Center. Licensed by O.B.P.V.S."

"A baby/teen/mom/dad, Powers Int'l/Images of St. Louis will be interviewing all sizes and ages who are interested in appearing in holiday advertisements and commercials in the Midwest. We are hired by producers in cooperations to find people for these types of assignments. Interviews: Saturday at the Marriott. No calls. Dress nice! We are licensed by the state of Missouri."

SAG Office: none

Film Commission: Mary Nell Clark, Director. Oklahoma Film Office 440 South Houston, Room 505, Tulsa, Oklahoma 74127; 918-581-2660; 800-766-3456; FAX 918-581-2844.

Department of Labor: 405-528-1500

OREGON
Does Oregon have a problem with entertainment scams? Yes.

April 23, 1992: Police arrested Christopher David Star (aka Chad Cadrecha and numerous other aliases) on allegations of sex abuse involving a man who responded to a newspaper classified advertisement seeking actors for a movie.

How are problems solved: Work with other film commissions. The Attorney General will become involved, if necessary.

Licensing: Oregon does not have specific laws regulating talent/modeling agencies. Employment agencies must be licensed by the Bureau of Labor. A written examination is required for a licensee.

An agency cannot operate out of a residence. An applicant for an agency license must have at least one year prior experience as an agent. Agencies must provide detailed and specific employment contracts. All advertising must contain the name and address of the agency. The symbol "$$$" cannot be used as a substitute for salary or earnings offered. Agencies can charge a maximum 5% commission. A bond is required in the amount of $5,000. There is an Employment Agencies Advisory Board.

Newspaper: The Sunday Oregonian

Published Disclaimer: None by publisher. The following notice was submitted and published: *"Actors. If you have questions regarding advertising for actors and/or production companies, you may call the Oregon State Film and Video Office."*

Sample Ads:
"Models. Focus Management out of Hollywood looking to test models for national and international bookings."

"Dancer $Audition$. No experience necessary. Up to $10/hr.+. Dance locally or travel."

"Dancers, Alaska. Round trip air plus accommodations."

Newspaper: The Statesman Journal

Published Disclaimer: None.

Sample ads:
"Showbiz! I'm Atkinson of Atkinson & Associates lead promotions and productions: A star is born: James Bond 007 has gone American, The World Festival, and more! Nobody does it better. Promoter, Producer, Director, and Star."

SAG Office: None.

Film Commission: David Woolson, Director, Oregon Film & Video Division, One World Trade Center, Suite 300/121 SW Salmon, Portland, Oregon 97204; 503-229-5832; FAX 503-222-5050

Bureau of Labor/Industries: 503-731-4074

PENNSYLVANIA
Does Pennsylvania have a problem with entertainment scams?
Yes.

How problems are solved: Media cooperation, educational efforts.

Licensing: Pennsylvania has specific laws regulating, "Theatrical or entertainment agencies." Theatrical or entertainment agencies are licensed as employment agencies. Employment agencies must be licensed by the Department of Labor. Agencies cannot operate in a private home, or in "a neighborhood deemed unsatisfactory by the Department." Agents must pass an examination. Agents must provide a written statement as to how long any employer has been in the theatrical business. Talent must be provided with detailed and specific job contracts. All advertising must contain the agency name, address, and the words "employment agency." Agencies cannot charge advance registration fees. Agencies cannot exceed a 10% commission for temporary placement. A bond is required in the amount of $3,000.

Newspaper: The Philadelphia Inquirer

Published Disclaimer: none.

Sample Ads:
"*Modeling/Acting. Do you have what it takes? John Casablanca's Modeling Center and Vineland Studios of Hollywood seek new faces for modeling, film, print, TV commercials and sitcoms. They will be at the Adams Mark Hotel, Sunday. Complimentary evaluation and testing. Experience is not necessary, training available.*"

"*Models/Actors. Karisma Modeling is currently seeking all types for music videos, tv shows, and movies. Children for print and commercials. Models for fashion shows and calendars. Petite and tall. No experience*

*necessary. Earn $50-$300/hr. Don't be shy, you may
have what we are looking for. Free evaluation. State
licensed and bonded. License #BWO124100."*

SAG Office: 230 S. Broad St., 10th Floor, Philadelphia, Pennsylvania 19102; 215-545-3150.

Film Commission: Ted Hanson, Director, Pennsylvania Film Burea, Forum Bldg., Room 449, Harrisburg, Pennsylvania 17120; 717-783-3456; FAX 717-234-4560.

Department of Labor/Industry: 717-787-4134

RHODE ISLAND
Does Rhode Island have a problem with entertainment scams?
No.

Licensing: Rhode Island does not have state laws regulating employment agencies (which includes talent/modeling agencies).

Newspaper: The Providence Journal

Published Disclaimer: . . . Truth in advertising is covered under the *Unfair Trade Practice and Consumer Production Act* which is enforced by the Attorney General's Division of Consumer Protection. This Division investigates consumer complaints against manufacturers, wholesalers and retailers as well as all forms of deceptive trade practice including misrepresentation in advertising. If you have a complaing or would like information, you may call either of the following numbers:

Providence:	277-2104
Anwhere in R.I:	1-800-852-7776

Sample ads:
*"Modeling: Model Search/Seminar. Wednesday, 8 PM,
Biltmore Hotel, Providence and Thursday, 8 PM,
Marriott Hotel, Newport. Mystique Models of NYC,
since 1981. Males and females, all heights and ages. Top
clients in N.E. and NYC."*

SAG Office: None.

Film Commission: Rick Smith, Director, Film & TV Office, Department of Economic Development, 7 Jackson Walkway, Providence, Rhode Island 02903; 401-277-3456; FAX 401-277-2601.

SOUTH CAROLINA
Does South Carolina have a problem with entertainment scams? Yes.

How are problems solved: Consumer Affairs.

Licensing: South Carolina does not have specific laws regulating talent/modeling agencies. "Personnel Placement Services" must be licensed by the Secretary of State. Personnel Placement Services cannot operate in a residence. Personnel Placement Services cannot impose advance registration fees.

All advertising must contain the service name and identification as an employment placement service. Out-of-state agencies doing business in South Carolina must also advertise in the same manner.

A bond is required in the amount of $25,000.

Newspaper: The State

Published Disclaimer: None

Sample Ads: None found.

SAG Office: None.

Film Commission: Isabel Hill, Director. South Carolina Film Office P.O. Box 927, Columbia, South Carolina 29202; 803-737-0490, FAX 803-737-0418.

Secretary of State: 803-734-2176.

SOUTH DAKOTA
Does South Dakota have a problem with entertainment scams? Some

How problems are solved: Attorney General.

Licensing: South Dakota does not have state laws regulating employment agencies (which includes talent/modeling agencies).

Newspaper: The Rapid City Journal

Published disclaimer: none.

Sample ad: none found.

Newspaper: The Argus Leader

Published Disclaimer: "All ads are subject to approval before publication. We reserve the right to edit, refuse, reject or cancel any ad at any time."

Sample Ads: none found.

SAG Office: none.

Film Commission: Gary Keller, Director. South Dakota Film Commission 711 East Wells Ave., Pierre, South Dakota 57501-3369; 605-773-3301; 800-952-3625; FAX 605-773-3256.

Regulatory agency: Not applicable.

TENNESSEE
Does Tennessee have a problem with entertainment scams? Yes.
How are problems solved: Cooperation with the media, an Information Agency, and networking with neighboring states.

Licensing: Tennessee does not have specific laws regulating talent/modeling agencies. "Personnel Services" must be licensed with the Department of Commerce. Agents cannot charge any advance fees. No bond is required.

Newspaper: The Tennessean

Published Disclaimer: "The Publishers reserve the right to edit or reject any advertising copy submitted for publication."

Sample Ads:
"*Models/Actors. Career Modeling/Talent Management has immediate openings for print and film.*"

SAG Office: 1108 17th Ave. South., Nashville, Tennessee 37212; 615-327-2958.

Film Commission: Dancy Jones, Director, Tennessee Film, Entertainment & Music Commission, 320 6th Avenue North, 7th Floor, Nashville, Tennessee 37243-0790; 615-741-3456; 800-251-8594; FAX 615-741-5829.

Personnel Recruiting Services Board: 615-741-4700

TEXAS
Does Texas have a problem with entertainment scams? Yes.

How problems are solved: Education efforts, referrals to professional associations, Better Business Bureau and the police if necessary. The state Department of Licensing distributes a caution to talent and models.

Licensing: Texas has specific laws which regulate "talent agencies." A talent agency must be licensed by the Department of Licensing and Regulation. Agencies cannot charge talent for advance registration fees, video or audio tapes, postcard service, advertising, resumes, photographs, classes, or require the subscription to a publication. All advertising must include the agency name, address, and license number. Agencies must pay talent "no later than 10 banking days" after the agency receives payment from the client. A bond is required in the amount of $10,000. The Department of Licensing publishes and distributes a helpful pamphlet entitled, "*Do You Want To Be An Actor Or A Model?*"

Newspaper: The Houston Chronicle

Published Disclaimer: "Employment Complaints: If you have a complaint, please remit it to the Better Business Bureau for action. Dial 868-9500, M-F 9 AM—4 PM, or write BBB, 2707 N. Loop West, No. 900, Houston, TX 77008."

Also:

"All advertising copy is accepted subject to the approval or rejection by the management of *The Houston Chronicle*. . .The Chronicle also reserves the right to edit, reject, or classify all ads under appropriate headings."

And under the classified heading, Theatrical/Movie/TV: "Some of the ads in this classification may require a fee."

Sample Ads:

---

773   THEATRICAL

ACTING
MODELING
A PROFESSION THAT'S
WORTH LOOKING INTO!

A model or actor can make as much money, if not more, than a computer scientist, a doctor, chemical engineer, or lawyer. And all ages are in. Females & Males.
ATTEND OUR SEMINAR:
"Looking Into Modeling & Acting"
Screen Test & Talent Analysis
555-8889

"Actors/Models. No experience necessary. Up to $50/hr. Talent Manager interviewing today. Lic. #223."

"A Model Search. Our Talent Managers are conducting an extensive model search this week for all ages throughout the Houston area. $50/hr. & up. Looking for real people and high fashion models looking to engage in catalogs, newspapers, fashion, print, TV, motion

pictures. *For personal interview call Talent Manager today."*

"Catalogue Models. Looking for catalogue models for major department stores and boutiques here in Houston. Females & males. Now test shooting. Call Talent Manager. Lic. #1870. Top Models Agency."

"Fame and Money. A seminar for people who want to break into modeling and acting. 'Get the Facts.' It's free. This Saturday. Bonjelle World Model Center."

"Fashion Show Models. Females and Males for weekly runway fashion shows. Auditions and screenings this Mon. & Tues. only. Top Model Agency. Lic. # 146."

Newspaper: The Dallas Morning News

Published Disclaimer: None.

Sample ads:
"Modeling Seminar. Learn the secrets of the glamorous and exciting world of modeling from Int'l Vogue Cover-Girl Model. Enrollment limited. $229. Call to schedule a preliminary interview."

"Female figure models needed, $100 paid per photo session."

"Dallas Model Group/Model Search. Open Call. Experience only, please. Women 5'7" or taller; men 6' or taller; 18-25 years. No exceptions. No phone calls. Bring nonreturnable photo."

SAG Offices: Two Dallas Communications Complex, 6309 North O'Connor Road, Suite 111-LB 25, Irving Texas 75039; 214-869-9400 and; 2650 Fountainview, Suite 326, Houston, Texas 77057; 713-972-1806.

Film Commission: Marlene Saritzky, Director, Texas Film Commission P.O. Box 13246, Austin, Texas 78711; 512-463-9200; FAX 512-463-4114.

Department of Licensing and Regulation: 512-463-2906

UTAH
Does Utah have a problem with entertainment scams? No.

Licensing: Utah does not have specific laws regulating talent/modeling agencies. Employment agencies must be licensed with the Industrial Commission. Employment agencies must provide detailed and specific employment contracts. Taking commissions or fees in advance is unlawful. "Positions listed in the 'Help Wanted' columns of the newspapers or other media shall refer to bona fide openings available at the time copy is given to those publications for insertion." A bond is required in the amount of $1,000.

Newspaper: Salt Lake Tribune

Published Disclaimer: "Newspapers have the right to edit, properly classify, cancel, or decline any ad." Also: "Notice. The advertisements appearing in this column may or may not constitute offers of employment. Persons responding to these advertisements may be required to pay fees in advance for licensing, permits, dues, portfolios, registration, processing, or other services. Opportunities advertised in this column may require training at the expense of the applicant. No guarantee of job availability, implied or direct, is made by the publishers."

Sample Ads:
   "Model/Actor Search. We're looking for FRESH NEW
   FACES and CHARACTER TYPES of all ages, for PRINT,
   VIDEOS, FILM.
   $ GREAT RATES $ No experience."

   "Casting Now! No experience—to pros, TV, movies,
   models, extras to $80/hr."

"Seriously looking at Modeling or Acting? Eastman Agency is an aggressive booking agency looking for print/runway models for top ski conventions, nat'l ads, TV, fashion shows. Actors needed for 4 motion picture productions. Experienced/no experience."

SAG Office: None.

Film Commission: Leigh von der Esch, Director. Utah Film Commission 324 South State Street, Suite 500, Salt Lake City, Utah 84111; 801-538-8740; 800-453-8824/FAX 801-538-888

Industrial Commission: 801-530-6800

VERMONT
Does Vermont have a problem with entertainment scams? No.

Licensing: Vermont does not have state laws regulating employment agencies (which includes talent/modeling agencies).

Newspaper: The Burlington Free Press

Published disclaimer: "The Burlington Free Press may edit, reject, or classify any advertising copy submitted by our customers."

Sample ads: None found.

SAG office: None.

Film Commission: Greg Gerdel, Director, Vermont Film Bureau, 134 State Street, Montpelier, Vermont 05602; 802-828-3237; FAX 802-828-3233.

Regulatory agency: Not applicable.

VIRGINIA
Does Virginia have a problem with entertainment scams? Yes.

How are problems solved: Education efforts, cooperation with all licensing authorities, and media and police involvement if necessary.

Licensing: Virginia does not have specific laws regulating talent/modeling agencies. Employment agencies must be licensed by the Department of Commerce. Agencies must provide detailed and specific contracts. All advertising must include the name and address of the agency. The symbol "$$$" cannot be used as a substitute for salary or job wage. A bond is required in the amount of $10,000.

Newspaper: Richmond Times-Dispatch

Published disclaimer: none.

Sample ads:
  "Actress sought, 20-30 for a 4-6 week special event marketing production. Must have experience in improv, crowd interaction and characterization. Great pay, 20-30 hrs/wk. Uniforms provided. Informal auditions will be held in Richmond. All ages, no children. All types/all ethnic groups. Please send headshot and resume. Calls accepted on Tuesday only, 1-508 . . . "

SAG Office: none.

Film Commission: Rita D. McClenny, Director, Virginia Film Office, P.O. Box 798, 1021 E. Cary Street, Suite 1200, Richmond, Virginia 23219; 804-371-8204, FAX 804-786-1121.

Department of Commerce: 804-367-8505

WASHINGTON D.C. *(See DISTRICT OF COLUMBIA)*

WASHINGTON
Does Washington have a problem with entertainment scams? No.

Licensing: Washington has specific laws regulating "Theatrical agencies." Theatrical agencies are licensed as employment agencies. Employment agencies must be licensed by the Department of Licensing. Agencies cannot charge or accept registration fees. All advertising "shall signify that it is an employment agency solicitation." Agency managers must pass a written exam. Commissions cannot lawfully exceed 20%. A bond is required in the amount of $2,000.

Newspaper: The Seattle Post-Intelligencer

Published disclaimer: "The position, subject matter, form, size, wording, illustrations and typography of all advertising are subject to the approval of Seattle Times Company which reserves the right to reposition, classify, edit, reject or cancel any advertisement at any time, before or after insertion."

Sample ads: none found.

Newspaper: *Tacoma Morning News Tribune*

Published disclaimer:

MORNING NEWS TRIBUNE
EMPLOYMENT ADVERTISING REGULATIONS

1. Each ad must clearly state what type of employment is being offered.
2. All advertised statements must be accurate and not designed to mislead the reader.
3. Commission only positions cannot run under Employment/Salary/Hourly.
4. Each ad must begin with a job position or by company name.
5. Employment agencies must state their name. If name does not include Personnel Agency, the words agency or fee must be in the ad. No Fee or Temporary Positions do not need agency or fee.
6. Employment requiring investment must run under Business Opportunities.

IT IS THE ADVERTISER'S RESPONSIBILITY TO BE AWARE OF FEDERAL, STATE AND LOCAL LAWS AND REGULATIONS PERTAINING TO EMPLOYMENT. IT IS THE MORNING NEWS TRIBUNE'S RIGHT TO REFUSE ALL ADVERTISEMENTS WHICH DO NOT COMPLY WITH THE ABOVE REGULATIONS.

Sample ads: None found.

SAG Office: 601 Valley St. #200, Seattle, 98109, 206-728-9999.

Film Commission: Christine Lewis, Director. Washington State Film & Video Office 2001 6th Ave., Suite 2600, Seattle, Washington 98121; 206-464-7148; FAX 206-464-5868.

Department of Licensing: 206-753-5029

WEST VIRGINIA
Does West Virginia have a problem with entertainment scams? No.

Licensing: West Virginia does not have specific laws regulating talent/modeling agencies. Employment agencies must be licensed by the Department of Labor. Monthly employment service reports must be filed with the Department of Labor. Agencies cannot accept advance registration fees exceeding $1 or require a subscription to a publication. Agencies cannot operate from residences. No bond is required.

Newspaper: Charleston Gazette-Mail

Published Disclaimer: none.

Sample Ads: none found.

SAG Office: none.

Film Commission: Jeff Harpold, Director, West Virginia Film Industry Development Office, P.O. Box 50315, 2101 Washington Street East, Charleston, West Virginia 25305-0315; 304-558-2286; 800-225-5982/FAX 304-558-0108.

Department of Labor: 304-588-7890

WISCONSIN
Does Wisconsin have a problem with entertainment scams? Yes.

How problems are solved: The Film Commission handles complaints on a case-by-case basis.

Licensing: Wisconsin has specific laws regulating modeling agencies, but not theatrical or booking agencies. Modeling agencies are licensed as employment agencies. Employment agencies must be licensed by the Department of Labor. Modeling agency commissions cannot exceed 15%. In addition to the 15% commission to talent, the modeling agency may charge talent "a service charge for specific services performed." A modeling agency must inform talent of excessive travel or the agency is liable for those expenses. A bond is required in the amount of $5,000.

Newspaper: The Milwaukee Journal

Published disclaimer: "*The Milwaukee Journal* reserves the right to correctly classify any advertisement, edit or delete any objectionable wording or reject any advertisement for credit or policy."

Sample ads:
"*Model Search. A Scout representing agencies in Milwaukee, Chicago and Minneapolis will be at S. 5th St., Thursday only. Women 5'7"-5'11", men 5'10"-6'3". New faces and all races encouraged to apply! For info call 1-(800)...*"

"*Models. Attractive models of all ages for advertising, photography and promotions. Celebrity doubles. Call after 7pm.*"

SAG office: none.

Film Commission: Stan Solheim, Director. Wisconsin Film Office 123 W. Washington, 6th Fl., P.O. Box 7970, Madison, Wisconsin, 53707; 608-267-3456; FAX 608-266-3403.

Department of Labor : 608-266-3345

WYOMING

Does Wyoming have a problem with entertainment scams? No.

Licensing: Wyoming does not have specific laws regulating talent/modeling agencies. Employment agencies must be licensed by the Department of Commerce. Agencies cannot charge registration fees of more than $2. A bond is required in the amount of $500.

Newspaper: Cheyenne Tribune-Eagle

Published disclaimer:

> **This news paper**
> recommends that you investigate every phase of business opportunities. We suggest that you consult your own attorney and ask for a free pamphlet or further information from the company making the offer before investing any money. Or, you may contact the Attorney General's Office, 123 Capitol Building, Cheyenne, WY 82002. 307/777-7841

Sample ads: None found.

SAG Office: None.

Film Commission: Bill Lindstrom, Director. Wyoming Film Commission I-25 & College Dr., Cheyenne, Wyoming, 82002-0240; 307-777-7777; 800-458-6657/FAX 307-777-6904.

Department of Labor: 307-777-7261

(ANADA

Two very active motion picture production areas in Canada are Vancouver, British Columbia (which some in the industry regard as "Hollywood North"), and Toronto, Ontario. Here is the same detailed information for those areas:

BRITISH COLUMBIA
Does British Columbia have problems with entertainment scams? Rarely.

How problems are solved: The film commission becomes personally involved. The police are involved, if necessary. A professional talent agent association is also utilized.

Licensing: British Columbia does not have specific laws regulating talent/modeling agencies. Employment agencies are regulated by the "Hiring Practices Act," through the Ministry of Labor. The city of Vancouver requires a city business license.

Newspaper: *The Vancouver Province*

Published Disclaimer: none.

Sample Ads:
"We're more than the #1 model agency in the world! John Casablanca's has been training students for the fashion, makeup and modeling industries since 1978.

Our graduates enjoy working both locally and internationally. Our personal development programs have helped thousands of young men and women gain the confidence and self esteem to make it in the '90s. Call today for more info on these exciting careers and courses. . . Makeup Artistry, Fashion Merchandising, Acting—Modeling, Personal Development. Call John Casablanca's Modeling and Fashion Career College."

"Talent Search. NIA Talent & Ze Models Int'l are looking for new faces for commercials, TV, film, print and fashion shows."

"Break into the movies. Extraordinary Casting needs extras now. Call!"

"We need movie extras! Call Extra Personalities."

Alliance of Canadian Cinema, Television, and Radio Artists: 1622 W. 7th Ave., Ste. #300, V6J 155, 604-734-1414.

Film Commission: Dianne Neufeld, Director, British Columbia Film Commission 601 W. Cordova St., Vancouver, V6B 1G1, British Columbia, CANADA; 604-660-2732; FAX 604-660-4790.

Ministry of Labor: 416-973-2311

ONTARIO

Does Ontario have a problem with entertainment scams? Yes.

December 11, 1992: *The Toronto Star reported "Fake 'Talent Scout' Admits Sex Attacks" . . . Selva Kumar Subbiah (aka "Richard Wild") was convicted of 14 counts of sexual assault after posing as a talent scout, then drugging his victims before having intercourse with some of them.*

How problems are solved: Referred to professional associations and/or police, if necessary.

Licensing: Ontario does not have specific laws regulating talent/modeling agencies. Employment agencies are regulated by the Hiring Practices Act, through the Ministry of Labor. Employment agencies cannot accept fees as a condition of employment. The city of Toronto does not require a business license.

Newspaper: The Toronto Sun

Published disclaimer: "*The Sun* reserves the right to refuse to accept or publish any advertisement that *The Sun* , in its sole discretion, deems objectionable or unacceptable. *The Sun* reserves the right to classify all advertisements. In consideration for the publication of any advertisement, the advertiser agrees to indemnify *The Sun* from any claims that arise out of a publication of such advertisement."

Sample ads:

MODELLING in Japan: min $10,000/ month for 2 mos. Tor. 555-9093. Scarb. 555-1144.

MOVIE Magic, fastest growing talent & extra agency reg. all nationalities & ages. Movies & commercials. Work guar. 555-5317.

Alliance of Canadian Cinema, Television & Radio Artists (National Office): 2239 Yonge St., Toronto, M4S 2B5, 416-489-1311.

Film Commission: Gail Thomson, Executive Coordinator. Ontario Film Development Corporation 175 Bloor St. East, Ste. #300, Toronto, M4W 3R8, 416-314-6858; FAX 416-314-6876.

Ministry of Labor: 416-973-2311

SUGGESTED READING

Invest in reference books. Start your own entertainment industry library. (Order catalogs from the booksellers listed here.)

ACTING/MODELING

Actor Be/Aware. Delores Chevron/FPA Agency, 4051 Radford Ave. #A, Studio City, CA 91604.

The Actor's & Models Source Directory. Heartbeat Enterprises, P.O. Box 570494, Tarzana, CA 91357.

The AFTRA-SAG Young Performers Handbook (call your nearest AFTRA or SAG office).

Back To One: How to Make Good Money as a Hollywood Extra. Cullen Chambers, Back To One Publications, P.O. Box 753-1, Hollywood, CA 90078-0753.

Child Modeling Scams: Parents Beware. Council of Better Business Bureaus, Inc., Public Affairs Dept., 4200 Wilson Blvd., Arlington, VA 22203.

Everything You Always Wanted to Know About L.A.'s and New York's Casting Directors. Wendy Shawn, Castbusters, P.O. Box 67C75, Los Angeles, CA 90067.

How To Get Into Commercials. Vangie Hayes, Harper and Row Publishers, 10 E. 53rd St., New York, NY 10022, 1983.

How To Get Work As A Movie Extra. 2nd Edition, Todd Worthington, Lone Eagle Publishing Co., 2337 Roscomare Rd. Suite 9, Los Angeles, CA 90077, 1991.

Models World Magazine. Midwest Publishing and Flair Communications, Inc. 1 Beekman St., New York, NY 10038.

Your Film Acting Career. Miki Lewis and Rosemary Lewis, Gorham House Publishing, 2210 Sunset Blvd., Suite 777, Santa Monica, CA 90403, 1989.

AGENTS/MANAGERS
Artist v. Manager v. Agent v. Labor Commission. Beverly Hills Bar Association, Entertainment Law Section, 1983.

Artist v. Manager Revisited . Richard R. Feller, Editor, Beverly Hills Bar Association, 1985.

Artist v. Manager Revisited. 2nd Edition, Richard L. Feller, Editor, Beverly Hills Bar Association, 1987.

Children's Agents & Managers Directory, Hollywood Screen Parents Association, P.O. Box 1612, Burbank, CA 91507-1612, 818-955-6510.

Hollywood Agents/Managers Directory. Hollywood Creative Directory, 3000 Olympic Blvd., #2413, Santa Monica, CA 90404, 1992.

The L.A. Agent Book. K. Callan, Sweden Press, P.O. Box 1612, Studio City, CA 91614, 1992.

Manager's, Entertainer's and Agent's Book. 2nd Revised Edition, Walter E. Hurst, Seven Arts Press, 6253 Hollywood Blvd., #1100, P.O. Box 649, Hollywood, CA 90028, 1980.

ASSOCIATIONS/ORGANIZATIONS

Academy of Motion Picture Arts and Sciences, 8949 Wilshire Blvd., Beverly Hills, CA 90211, 310-247-3000.

Academy of Motion Picture & Television Producers, 14144 Ventura Blvd., Sherman Oaks, CA 91423, 818-995-3600.

Academy of Television Arts and Sciences, 5220 Lankershim Blvd., N. Hollywood, CA 91601, 818-754-2800.

Association of Talent Agents, 9255 Sunset Blvd. #318, Los Angeles, CA 90069, 310-274-0628.

Casting Society of America, 6565 Sunset Blvd. #306, Los Angeles, CA 90028, 213-463-1925.

Conference of Personal Managers, Inc., c/o P.O. Box 8892, Universal City, CA 91608, 310-275-2456.

Council of Better Business Bureaus, 4200 Wilson Blvd., Arlington, VA 22203, 703-276-0100.

Hollywood Better Business Bureau, 3400 W. 6th St. #403, Los Angeles, CA 90020, 213-251-9696.

Hollywood Chamber of Commerce, 7000 Hollywood Blvd. #1, Hollywood, CA 90028, 213-469-8311.

Hollywood Screen Parents Association, P.O. Box 1612, Burbank, CA 91507-1612, 818-955-6510.

National Conference of Personal Managers, 210 E. 51st St., New York, New York 10022.

The Network, P.O. Box 85522, Los Angeles, CA 90072, 310-841-4889.

Women In Film, 6464 Sunset Blvd. #900, Hollywood, CA 90028, 213-463-6040.

INDUSTRY BOOKSTORES

Larry Edmunds Cinema and Theatre Bookshop, 6644 Hollywood Blvd., Los Angeles, CA 90028.

Samuel French Theatre and Film Bookshops, 7623 Sunset Blvd., Hollywood, CA 90046; 11963 Ventura Blvd., Studio City, CA 91604

Elliot M. Katt Bookseller, 8568 Melrose Ave., Los Angeles, CA 90069.

GENERAL

A Basic Guide to Exporting. U.S. Department of Commerce, 1-800-USA-TRADE.

Academy Players Directory. Academy of Motion Picture Arts & Sciences, 8949 Wilshire Blvd., Beverly Hills, CA 90211, 310-247-3000.

Beauty Queen Killer. Bruce Gibney, Windsor Publishing Corp., 475 Park Avenue South, New York, NY 10016, 1984.

The Complete Film Dictionary. Ira Konigsberg, Meridian/ Penguin Group, 375 Hudson St., New York, New York 10014, 1987.

The Hollywood Job Hunter's Survival Guide, Lone Eagle Publishing Company, 2337 Roscomare Road, Suite 9, Los Angeles, CA 90077, 1993

Hollywood Reporter Blubook. Hollywood Reporter, 6715 Sunset Blvd., Hollywood, CA 90028.

Hollywood Screen Parents News. Hollywood Screen Parents Association, 4720 N. Vineland Ave. #235, N. Hollywood, CA 91602, 818-955-6510.

How To Make It In Hollywood. Linda Buzzell, HarperCollins Publishers, Inc., 10 E. 53rd St., New York, New York 10022, 1992.

Law & Business of the Entertainment Industries. 2nd Edition. Biederman, Pierson, Silfer, Glasser, Berry, Praeger Publishing, 1 Madison Ave., New York, NY 10010, 1992.

Locations. Association of Film Commissioners International, c/o Utah Film Commission, 324 S. State St. #500, Salt Lake City, Utah 84111, 801-538-0540.

Monologues They Haven't Heard. Roger Karshner, Dramaline Publications, 10470 Riverside Dr. #201, Toluca Lake, CA 91602, 1987.

Pacific Coast Studio Directory. Pacific Coast Studio Directories, P.O. Box 5347, Pine Mountain, CA 93222-5347.

PRODUCTION DIRECTORIES
(Available from most film commissions.)

Screen Actor. Screen Actors Guild, 7065 Hollywood Blvd., Los Angeles, CA 90028-6065.

Screen Actor Hollywood. Screen Actors Guild (newsletter), 7065 Hollywood Blvd., Los Angeles, CA 90028-6065.

The Studio Teachers Blue Book. International Alliance of Theatrical Stage Employees (check your local union).

UNIONS & GUILDS (U.S.)
American Federation of Television & Radio Artists (AFTRA) 6922 Hollywood Blvd./P.O. Box 4070, Hollywood, CA 90078, 213-461-8111; 260 Madison Ave./7th Fl., New York, NY 10016, 212-532-0800.

Casting Society of America (CSA) 6565 Sunset Blvd., #306, Los Angeles, CA 90028, 213-463-1925.

Directors Guild of America (DGA) 7920 Sunset Blvd., Los Angeles, CA 90046, 310-289-2000; 213-851-3671; 110 W. 57th St., New York, NY 10019, 212-581-0370.

Producers Guild of America (PGA)
400 S. Beverly Dr., Suite 211, Beverly Hills, CA 90212, 310-465-4600.

Screen Actors Guild (SAG)
5757 Wilshire Blvd., Hollywood, CA 90028, 213-465-4600.

1515 Broadway/44th Fl., New York, NY 10036, 212-827-1474/212-944-6797.

Studio Teachers-Welfare Workers
Los Angeles Local #884, P.O. Box 461467, Los Angeles, CA 90046, 213-650-3792.

UNIONS & GUILDS (CANADA)
Alliance of Canadian Cinema, Television & Radio Artists
2239 Yonge St., Toronto, Ontario M4S 2B5, 416-489-1435.

Directors Guild of Canada (DGC)
387 Bloor St. East, Suite 401, Toronto, Ontario M4W 1H7, 416-972-6058.

PAGEANTS
Beauty Pageants: Tots to Teens." Mary Consentino and Paulette Vrett, Coznik and Co., St. Paul, MN 55113, 1991.

Becoming a Beauty Queen. Barbara Peterson Burwell and Polly Peterson Bowles, Prentice Hall Press, 1 Gulf and Western Plaza, New York, New York 10023, 1987.

Ms. America Through the Looking Glass. Nanice S. Martin, Messner Books, 1230 Avenue of the Americas, New York, NY 10020, 1985.

Miss America: In Pursuit of the Crown. Ann-Marie Bivans, Mastermedia Ltd., 1991.

Pageantry Magazine. Charles Dunn, Publisher, P.O. Box 160307, Altamonte Springs, FL 32716, 407-260-2262.

Tiara: An Insider's Guide to Choosing and Winning Pageants. Barbara Thompson Howell, Tiara Publications, P.O. Box 305, Whippany, NJ 07981, 1992.

TRADE PUBLICATIONS

Back Stage, B.P.I. Publications, 1515 Broadway, 14th Fl., New York, NY 10036, 212-764-7300.

Back Stage/West, B.P.I. Publications, 2035 Westwood Blvd. #210, Los Angeles, CA 90025, 310-474-6161.

Dramalogue. Billboard, Inc., P.O. Box 38771, Los Angeles, CA 90038, 213-464-5079.

Daily Variety. Cahners Publishing Co., 5700 Wilshire Blvd. #120, Los Angeles, CA 90036, 213-857-6600.

Hollywood Reporter. Hollywood Reporter, Inc., 5055 Wilshire Blvd., Los Angeles, CA 90036, 213-525-2000.

INDEX

M
Madison Square Garden Events 37
Madonna 31
Mail order 32
Maine 135
  Bangor Daily News 135
  Maine Telegram 135
Managers 57
Maryland 136
  Baltimore Sun 136
Massachusetts 137
Masschusetts
  Boston Globe 137
McDermott, Kevin 63
MCI 44
Michigan 138
  Detroit Free Press 138
Midgen, Chester L. 70
Minnesota 139
  Star-Tribune 139
Miss Glamour America Beauty and Talent Pageant 37
Miss Teen USA 37
Miss Universe 37
Miss USA 37
Missing Persons 95
Mississippi 140
  Clarion Ledger 141
Missouri 141
  St. Louis Post-Dispatch 141
Model Release 72
Model Release and Consent Agreement 50
Model Searches 38, 46
  Admission fees 38
Modeling
  Lingerie 11
Modeling Requirements
  Height and Age 81
Models 6
  Bathing suit 21
Modems 35

Monologue 1
Montana 142
  Billings Gazette 143

N
National Conference of Personal Managers 69
National Fraud Hotline 110
National Fraud Information Center 95
Nebraska 143
  Lincoln Journal-Star 143
Network, The 66
Nevada 108, 144
  Las Vegas 10
  Las Vegas Review-Journal 145
Nevada, Henderson 11
New Hampshire 146
  Colebrook 8
  Manchester Union 146
New Jersey 147
  Star-Ledger 147
New Mexico 148
  Albuquerque Journal 148
New York 149
  New York Times 149
Norris, Chuck 34
North Carolina 150
  Raleigh News and Observer 150
North Dakota 151
  Bismark Tribune 151
Nude
  Photography 9
    Consent for 9
  Posing of 11

O
Offers
  Too good to be true 41
Ohio 151
  Plain Dealer 151
Oklahoma 153
  Oklahoman 153

OTHER FILM BOOKS FROM
LONE EAGLE PUBLISHING CO.

CALL 1 800 FILMBKS TO ORDER

THE HOLLYWOOD JOB HUNTER'S
SURVIVAL GUIDE
**An Insider's Winning Strategies For Getting
That (all-important) First Job ...And Keeping It**
HUGH TAYLOR
$16.95
ISBN 0-943728-51-7, 314 pp, illustrations

There are currently over 250,000 students taking film courses
in colleges and universities in the United States. Many of them
will be making their way to Hollywood to try to get a job in
"the business." For those of you who have no "uncle in pro-
duction," "a cousin who's a director," "or a friend at the studio," Taylor offers insider's
advice on getting that all-important first job in the entertainment industry.
Taylor's well-written guide discusses Getting The Job, Setting up the Office and Getting To Work, The Script and Story Development Process, Production, Information,
Putting It all Together, Issues and Perspectives.

HUGH TAYLOR recently received his MBA in Business from Harvard's School of Business Administration. He has worked for the past two summers as an assistant to one of
Hollywood's top producers moving up from the job of "gofer" to his current position as
a development executive. In his tenure at his job, he has come up with his strategies for
finding the right job and keeping it.

SCREEN ACTING
How To Succeed in Motion Pictures and Television
BRIAN ADAMS
$15.95
ISBN 0-943728-20-7, 6 x 9, 378 pp, illustrations

This comprehensive and practical guide to motion picture and television acting
covers personal presentation, acting development and performance techniques for
the camera. Fully illustrated, it discusses preparing audition tapes, securing an agent,
selecting an acting school, handling screen tests and readings, working with
directors, and much more.

FILM SCHEDULING
Or, How Long Will It Take To Shoot Your Movie?
Second Edition

RALPH S. SINGLETON
$19.95
ISBN 0-943728-39-8, 240 pages, full-color fold-out production
board

"Detailing step-by-step how one creates a production board, shot-by-shot, day-by-day, set-by-set to turn a shooting schedule into a workable production schedule... For every film production student and most professionals."

—*Los Angeles Times*

The highly respected and best-selling book by Emmy award-winning producer Ralph Singleton. FILM SCHEDULING contains a new section on computerized film scheduling. This section not only analyzes and compares the various computer programs which are currently on the market but also instructs the reader on how to maintain personal control over the schedule while taking advantage of the incredible speed a computer offers. The definitive work on film scheduling.

FILM BUDGETING
Or, How Much Will It Cost to Shoot Your Movie?
RALPH S. SINGLETON
$22.95
ISBN 0-943728-65-7,approx. 300 pp, illustrated,
Includes full theatrical feature budget.

"Read FILM BUDGETING if you want to know how budgets are done in Hollywood. Singleton is a pro who has written a common-sense , nuts-and-bolts book complete with detailed explanations and illustrations."

—*Michael Hill, VP Production, Paramount Pictues*

The companion book to the best-sellingFILM SCHEDULING and its workbook (THE FILM SCHEDULING/FILM BUDGETING WORKBOOK), **FILM BUDGETING**takes the reader through the steps of converting a professional motion picture schedule to a professional motion picture budget. Using Francis Coppola's Academy Award nominated screenplay, *The Conversation*, as the basis for the examples, author Singleton explains the philosophy behind motion picture budgeting as well as the mechanics. Readers do not have to be computer-literate to use this text, although computer budgeting is discussed.

Included are a complete motion picture budget to *The Conversation* , as well as footnotes, glossary and index. When used in conjunction with its companion workbook, THE FILM SCHEDULING/FILM BUDGETING WORKBOOK, **FILM BUDGETING** can comprise a do-it-yourself course on motion picture budgeting.

FILM SCHEDULING FILM BUDGETING WORKBOOK
Ralph S. Singleton
Do-It-Yourself Guide
$19.95
ISBN 0-943728-07-X, 9 x 11, 296 pp

ALL SHEETS PERFORATED

Complete DO-IT-YOURSELF workbook companion to *Film Scheduling* and *Film Budgeting*.)
Contains the entire screenplay to Francis Coppola's Academy Award nominated screenplay, *THE CONVERSATION*, as well as sample production and budget forms to be completed
by the reader.

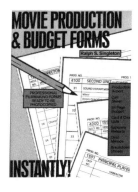

MOVIE PRODUCTION AND BUDGET FORMS...INSTANTLY!
Ralph S. Singleton
$19.95
ISBN 0-943728-14-2, 9 x 12, 132 pp

PROFESSIONAL FORMS
ALL SHEETS PERFORATED

INCLUDES
Call Sheet • Production Report • Breakdown Sheets
• Deal Memos • 84-page Feature Budget Form, and
more.
This book plus one photocopy machine equals every
production and budget form needed to make a full-
length feature or telefilm. Completely re-designed and
integrated forms that are 8.5" x 11" format, ready to
tear out and use over and over again.

FILMMAKER'S DICTIONARY
Ralph S. Singleton
$12.95
ISBN 0-943728-08-8, 6 x 9, 188 pp
Over 1500 Film Terms, Words,
Vocabulary, Phrases, Jargon,
Expressions and Definitions

*"So you don't know what pups, snoots, kooks, high hats, velociators and wigwags are? Look
them up in the Filmmaker's Dictionary, a marvelously comprehensive book that offers concise
nuts and bolts definitions of technical and legal terms used in scripts, contracts and every aspect
of production and distribution. Also included are definitions for on-set slang and tradepaper
jargon, the different professions and organizations and acronyms. Indispensable...."*
                                                                    —LIBRARY JOURNAL

THE LANGUAGE OF VISUAL EFFECTS

Micheal J. McAlister
$18.95
ISBN 0-943728-47-9, 4.5 x 8.5, 176 pp
illustrations, hologram on cover

"...for people in the technical side of the business as well as for those in the academic arena."
—*George Lucas*

"Oscar-winning effects artist Micheal McAlister has provided the perfect reference to provide a comprehensive listing of hundreds of effects terms with concise explanations understandable to the layman. It will be a pleasure to refer my readers to this valuable volume.
—*Don Shay, Editor/Publisher, Cinefex Magazine*

"A visual effects 'Bible' that will soon be in every filmmaker's library as an excellent reference guide to visual effects work."
—*Tom Joyner, Executive Production Manager/Feature Production,*
Warner Bros., Inc.

MICHEAL J. MCALISTER is recognized as one of the industry's top Visual Effects Supervisors. He spent eleven years at Lucasfilm's Industrial Light and Magic where he garnered an Academy Award, an Emmy, a British Academy Award, a second Academy Award nomination and a second British Academy Award nomination. His work has been the subject of many television reports including *Entertainment Tonight, The Today Show, Nova* and various documentary specials both in the United States and abroad.

THE FILM EDITING ROOM HANDBOOK

How To Manage The Near Chaos of the Cutting Room
NORMAN HOLLYN
$22.95
ISBN 0-943728-33-9, 6 x 9
445 pp, illustrations, bibliography, index

A well-written, semi-technical and profusely illustrated book which covers the editing process from pre-production image and sound, opticals, mixing and music editing through post-production answer print and previews. Perhaps most important, Hollyn tells how to get an editing job. An experienced editor who has worked on *Fame, Hair, Lenny, Network, Heathers* and, most recently, *Jersey Girl*, Hollyn knows his subject well. A book for movie fans as well as specialists.

192

TOP SECRETS: SCREENWRITING
Jurgen Wolff and Kerry Cox
$19.95
ISBN 0-943728-50-9, 6 x 9, 342 pp

TOP SECRETS: SCREENWRITINGoffers the professional and novice writer alike in-depth advice from top screenwriters in the industry. Each chapter is broken down into four parts: 1) an essay detailing the writer's background, discussing the impace and importance of the writer's work; 2) an extensive and probing interview giving the reader information not only to unlock the secrets of these scripts, but also helpful guidance; 3) a synopsis of the screenplay; and 4) the scene which the writer feels is the most important or entertaining. These scenes are presented in script format with the original stage directions. Featured are: Michael Blake (*Dances With Wolves*); Jim Cash (*Top Gun*); Nicholas Kazan (*Reversal of Fortune*); Tom Schulman (*Dead Poets Society*); Mary Agnes Donoghue (*Paradise*); and others.

SILENT PICTURES
Katie Maratta
$9.95
ISBN 0-943728-49-5, 7 x 8

Early buzz on **Silent Pictures**:
"You don't have to be a genius to make fun of Hollywood."
—Katie's husband
"All my children have nice features."
—Katie's mom

Hot from the pages of *Calendar,* the Los Angeles <u>Times'</u> answer to *Daily Variety* and *The Hollywood Reporter*, comes Katie Maratta's **Silent Pictures**. Her witty, incisive and often biting cartoons have given the film industry something to laugh at, paste on bulletin boards, fax to others and generally wish they had authored. Now for the first time, Maratta's most popular cartoons are assembled here in book form. Great for gifts!

KATIE MARATTA draws a Hollywood cartoon for the Los Angeles <u>Times</u>.

Annual
Reference Directories

1. **Film Directors: A Complete Guide** $50
2. **Film Writers Guide** $45
3. **Film Producers, Studios, Agents &**
    Casting Directors Guide $45
4. **Cinematographers, Production Designers,**
    Costume Designers & Editors Guide $45
5. **Special Effects & Stunts Guide** $45
6. **Film Composers Guide** $45
7. **Film Actors Guide** $50
8. **Television Writers Guide** $45
9. **Television Directors Guide** $45
10. **Film Distribution Guide** $125
    (INCLUDES BOXOFFICE, **MPAA**
    RATINGS, GENRE CODES,
    RELEASING INFORMATION, AND
    MORE, FOR OVER **2,000** FILMS
    FROM **1986-1992)**

    New Directory

THESE CREDIT AND CONTACT DIRECTORIES FEATURE:

- Working professionals of the film and television industry
- Contact information
- Credits
- Releasing information (date/studio or date/network)
- Academy & Emmy Awards & nominations
- Index of Names
- Index of Film (Television) Titles, cross-referenced (except Actors)
- Index of Agents & Managers
- Interviews (selected volumes)
- and more

Call 1 800 FILMBKS
FOR CURRENT EDITIONS AND PRICES.

How To Order

1. **CALL 1-800-FILMBKS.** Have your credit card ready (Visa, MC or American Express.) Your order will be taken and your books shipped to you ASAP. We usually ship by UPS Ground, but other arrangements can be made.

2. **MAIL** us your request with a check, money order or credit card information. California residents add in 8.25% sales tax. All orders should add in shipping charges: $4.00 fir first book, $1.50 each additional book. Do not forget to put expiration date and sign the request. Include your phone number. Our mailing address is:

   LONE EAGLE PUBLISHING CO.
   Dept. GS
   2337 Roscomare Road, Suite 9
   Los Angeles, CA 90077-1851
   310/471-8066

3. **FAX** us your request with all the information listed above. Our fax is **310/471-4969.**

ABOUT THE AUTHOR

Erik Joseph has researched thousands of glam scams. From the "producer" who claimed he couldn't obtain the proper permit because he was dyslexic, to the fraudulent "entertainment attorney" who vehemently defended his unlicensed "agent" client, to the male model who wanted to know if the "photographer" who wanted the young man to strip naked and wear a dog collar was legit.

Trained as a talent agent in Hollywood and ripped-off as a fledgling actor/model, Joseph currently consults with enforcement officials across the country.

Erik Joseph is Assistant Director for the Nevada state film office. He conducts glam scam workshops and seminars and periodically teaches Continuing Education classes at the University of Nevada, Las Vegas. He has directed various entertainment industry studies and authored numerous articles on talent and model scams for such publications as *Location Magazine, Daily Variety, The Hollywood Reporter, Backstage West, the Las Vegas Review-Journal-Sun.* Consumer ombudsman David Horowitz has featured ErikJoseph on CNBC's "Steals and Deals talking about how to protect oneself from "Glam Scams." At times, Erik has found it necessary to go undercover as the "naive model/actor," the "inquisitive parent" or the "indifferent boyfriend."

Born and raised in Dearborn, Michigan, Erik now lives in Las Vegas, Nevada. He has a B.A. from Fresno State University, Fresno, California, and an M.A. in film studies from Wayne State University, in Detroit, Michigan.